Guiding Those Left Behind
In Florida

LEGAL AND PRACTICAL THINGS
YOU NEED TO DO
TO SETTLE AN ESTATE IN FLORIDA

and

HOW TO ARRANGE YOUR OWN AFFAIRS
TO AVOID UNNECESSARY COSTS
TO YOUR FAMILY

By Florida Attorney
AMELIA E. POHL

EAGLE PUBLISHING COMPANY OF BOCA

The purpose of this book is to provide the reader with an informative overview of the subject; but laws change frequently and are subject to different interpretations as courts rule on the meaning or effect of a law. This book is sold with the under-standing that neither the authors, nor the editors, nor the publisher, nor the distributors of this book are engaging in, or rendering, legal, accounting, financial planning, or any other professional service. If you need legal, accounting, financial planning or any other expert advice, you should seek the services of a licensed professional.

This book is intended for use by the consumer for his or her own benefit. If you use this book to counsel someone about the law or tax matters, then that may be considered to be an unauthorized and illegal practice.

WEB SITES: Web sites appear throughout the book. These Web sites are offered for the convenience of the reader only. Publication of these Web site addresses is not an endorsement by the authors, editors or publishers of this book.

EAGLE PUBLISHING COMPANY OF BOCA
4199 N. Dixie Highway, #2
Boca Raton, FL   33431   E-mail: info@eaglepublishing.com

Printed in the United States of America
ISBN 1932464069
Library of Congress Catalog Card Number 2004116794

Guiding Those Left Behind In Florida

CONTENTS

About The Book

We tried to make this book as comprehensive as possible so there are specialized sections of the book that do not apply to the general population and may not be of interest to you. The following GUIDE POSTS appear throughout the book. You can read the section if the situation applies to you or skip the section if it doesn't. Skipping the section will not affect the continuity of the book.

GUIDE POSTS

The SPOUSE POST means that the information provided is specifically for the spouse of the decedent. If the decedent was single, you can skip this section.

The CALL-A-LAWYER POST alerts you to a situation that may require the assistance of an attorney. See the end of this chapter for information about how to find a lawyer.

The CAUTION POST alerts you to a potential problem. It is followed by a suggestion about how to avoid the problem.

The SPECIAL SITUATION POST means that the information given in that paragraph applies to a particular event or situation; for example when the decedent dies a violent death. If the situation does not apply, you can skip the section.

The Organization of the Book

Guiding Those Left Behind refers to the things that need to be done in order to settle an Estate in Florida. The purpose of this book is to guide the reader through that process. It explains:

1. How to tend to the funeral and burial
2. What agencies need to be notified
3. How to locate the decedent's property
4. What bills need (and do not need) to be paid
5. How to determine who is entitled to inherit the decedent's property
6. How to transfer the decedent's property to the proper beneficiary

We devoted a chapter to each of these 6 steps; and for those who are in charge of settling an Estate, we placed a CHECK LIST at the end of Chapter 6 summarizing the things that need to be done. Once you read Chapters 1 through 6 you will be able to identify those problems that can happen when someone dies. Using those Chapters as a base, you can set up your own Estate Plan so that your family is not burdened by similar problems. The rest of the book (Chapters 7, 8 and 9) suggests different strategies you can use to accomplish this goal.

GLOSSARY

This book is designed for the average reader. Legal terminology has been kept to a minimum. There is a glossary at the end of the book in the event you come across a legal term that is not familiar to you.

FICTITIOUS NAMES AND EVENTS

The examples in this book are based loosely on actual events; however, all names are fictitious; and the events, as portrayed, are fictitious.

Reading the Law

Where applicable, we identified the state statute federal statute that is the basis of the discussion. We did this as a reference, and also to encourage the reader to look at the law as it is written. Prior to the Internet the only way you could look up the law was to physically take yourself to the local courthouse law library or the law section of a public library. Today all of the state and federal statutes are literally at your finger tips. They are just a mouse click away on the Internet. To look up a statute all you need is the address of the Web site and the identifying number of the statute.

FEDERAL STATUTES
http://www4.law.cornell.edu/uscode

FLORIDA STATUTES
http://www.leg.state.fl.us

The Florida legislature organized their laws into some 985 Chapters. Each Chapter is divided into numbered sections. We will identify the statute by its Chapter and Section. For example, (FS 700.14) refers to Chapter 700, Section 14 of the Florida Statutes. To look up a statute, go to the Web site, find the title and then the section within the title.

You may find it both interesting and profitable to read the law as it is actually written, if you come across a topic in the book that is important to you.

Amelia E. Pohl, Esq.

Before becoming an attorney in 1985, AMELIA E. POHL taught mathematics on both the high school and college level. During her tenure as Associate Professor of Mathematics at Prince George's Community College in Maryland, she wrote several books including
Probability: A Set Theory Approach
Principals of Counting
Common Stock Sense.

During her practice of law Attorney Pohl observed that many people want to reduce the high cost of legal fees by performing or assisting with their own legal transactions. Attorney Pohl found that, with a bit of guidance, people are able to perform many legal transactions for themselves. Attorney Pohl utilizes her background as teacher, author and attorney to provide that "bit of guidance" to the general public in the form of self-help legal books that she has written. Amelia E. Pohl is currently "translating" this book for the remaining 49 states:
Guiding Those Left Behind in Maine
Guiding Those Left Behind In North Dakota
Guiding Those Left Behind In Wyoming, etc.

THE DESIGN ARTIST

LUBOSH CECH designed the cover of this book. He is a renowned artist, with extensive educational background and professional work experience. He studied design, applied art, and painting in his native Prague, Czech Republic. Just before graduating from the Ph.D. program in art history at the Charles University in Prague, he defected to Italy to escape the political persecution of the communist government. While in Italy, he studied at the University of Bologna.

Since moving to the United States in 1984, Mr. Cech has been designing art exhibitions, working as an art director, and graphic designer. Mr. Cech is a photographer and often incorporates his photographs into his art work.

Lubosh Cech is the founder of OKO DESIGN STUDIO located in Portland, Oregon. He designs promotional materials for print and digital media. He has received numerous rewards for both graphic design and painting. For more information about Mr. Cech and the OKO Design Studio visit his Web site.

http://www.okodesignstudio.com

THE PHOTOGRAPHER

The photograph that appears on the cover was taken by photographer GENE OSON.

ACKNOWLEDGMENT

When someone dies, the family attorney is often among the first to be called. Family members have questions about whether probate is necessary, who to notify, how to get possession of the assets, etc. Over the years, as I practiced in the field of Elder Law, I noticed that the questions raised were much the same family to family. I thought a book answering such questions would be of service to the general public.

I also observed, that those who had experience in settling the Estate of a loved one were more understanding of the process, and better able to make decisions about how to arrange their own finances to avoid problems that could arise in settling an Estate. The "Guiding" in the title of this book refers to the guidance given in the event that you need to settle the Estate of your loved one. It also refers to the guidance that you can give to your family by setting up your own Estate Plan so that your family is not burdened by unnecessary costs and delays in settling your Estate.

I wish to thank all of the clients, who I have had the honor and pleasure to serve, for providing me with the impetus to produce this book.

When You Need A Lawyer

The purpose of this book is to give the reader a basic understanding of Florida law as it relates to Wills and other methods of Estate Planning. It is not intended as a substitute for legal counsel or any other kind of professional advice. If you have a legal question, you should seek the counsel of an attorney. When looking for an attorney, consider three things:
EXPERTISE, COST and PERSONALITY.

EXPERTISE

The Florida Bar has a certification program for 19 different areas of law including BUSINESS LITIGATION, CIVIL TRIAL, ELDER LAW, WILLS, TRUST AND ESTATES. To be certified by the Florida Bar as a specialist in these areas, the attorney must have practiced in that area of law for a number of years (usually 5) and pass a comprehensive Florida Bar Certification Examination.

The Florida Bar has a STATEWIDE REFERRAL SERVICE. You can call them at (800) 342-8011 and ask for a referral to an attorney in your county who is experienced in the area of law that you seek. The Florida Bar has a Web site that give the name and telephone numbers of all of the Board Certified Attorneys in the state of Florida.

THE FLORIDA BAR
http://www.flabar.org

Certification is just one of the criteria to consider. Many fine attorneys are experienced in an area of law, but the attorney may not have taken the time, effort or expense to become certified as a specialist. If the attorney is not certified in the branch of law you seek, ask how long he has practiced that type of law and what percentage of his practice is devoted to that branch of law.

One of the most reliable ways to find an attorney is through personal referral. Ask your friends, family or business acquaintances if they used an attorney for the field of law that you seek and whether they were pleased with the results. It is important to employ an attorney who is experienced in the area of law you seek. Your friend may have a wonderful Estate Planning attorney, but if you suffered an injury to your body, you need an attorney experienced in Personal Injury.

Before employing an attorney for a job, ask how long he has practiced that type of law and what percentage of his practice is devoted to that type of law.

COST

In addition to the attorney's experience, it is important to check what it will cost in attorney's fees. When you call for an appointment ask what the attorney will charge for the initial consultation and the approximate cost for the service you seek. Ask whether there will be additional costs such as filing fees, accounting fees, expert witness fees, etc.

If the least expensive attorney is out of your price range then you can call your local county Bar Association for the telephone number of the Legal Aid office nearest you or you can call the Statewide Referral Service at (800) 342-8011 for the telephone number.

The American Bar Association has a directory of Florida Legal Services Programs at the General Public Resources section of its Web site.

THE AMERICAN BAR ASSOCIATION
http://www.abanet.org

PERSONALITY

Of equal importance to the attorney's experience and legal fees, is your relationship with the attorney. How easy was it to reach the attorney? Did you go through layers of receptionists and legal assistants before being allowed to speak to the attorney? Did the attorney promptly return your call? If you had difficulty reaching the attorney, then you can expect similar problems should you employ that attorney.

Did the attorney treat you with respect? Did the attorney treat you paternally with a "father knows best" attitude or did he treat you as an intelligent person with the ability to understand the options available to you and the ability to make your own decision based on the information provided to you?

Are you able to understand and easily communicate with the attorney? Is he speaking to you in plain English or is his explanation of the matter so full of legalese to be almost meaningless to you?

Do you find the attorney's personality to be pleasant or grating? Sometimes people rub each other the wrong way. It is like rubbing a cat the wrong way. Stroking a cat from head to tail is pleasing to the cat, but petting it in the opposite direction, no matter how well intended, causes friction. If the lawyer makes you feel annoyed or uncomfortable, then find another attorney.

It is worth the effort to take the time to interview as many attorneys as it takes to find one with the right expertise, fee schedule and personality for you.

The First Week

Dealing with the death of a close family member or friend is difficult. Not only do you need to deal with your own emotions, but often with those of your family and friends. Sometimes their sorrow is more painful to you, than what you are experiencing yourself.

In addition to the emotional impact of a death, there are many things that need to be done, from arranging the funeral and burial, to closing out the business affairs of the *decedent* (the person who died) and finally giving whatever property is left to the proper beneficiary.

The funeral and burial take only a few days. Wrapping up the affairs of the decedent may take considerably longer. This chapter explains what things you (the spouse or closest family member) need to do during the first week, beginning at the moment of death and continuing through the funeral.

 MALE GENDER USED

Rather than use "he/she" or "his/her" for simplicity
(and hoping not to offend anyone)
we will refer to the decedent and his
Personal Representative using the male gender.

References to other people will be in both genders.

AUTOPSIES

In today's high tech world of medicine, doctors are fairly certain of the cause of death, but if there is a question, the family may be asked for permission to perform an autopsy. If, during his lifetime, the decedent appointed a HEALTH CARE SURROGATE (someone to make his medical decisions) he can give written permission for the procedure. If no Surrogate was appointed, the spouse or nearest relative may give consent (FS 872.04 (2)).

The person who authorizes the autopsy must agree to pay for it because the cost of the examination is not covered under most health insurance plans. And that cost could be sizeable, running anywhere from several hundred to several thousand dollars, but it is in the family's best interest to consent to the autopsy. The examination might reveal a genetic disorder that could be treated if it later appears in another family member. Death from a car "accident" could have been a heart attack at the wheel. Perhaps the patient who died suddenly in a hospital was misdiagnosed. The nursing home resident could have died from negligence and not old age. Even if none of these are found, knowing the cause of death with certainty is better than not knowing.

That was the case with the family of a woman who was taken to the hospital complaining of stomach pains. The doctors thought she might be suffering from gallbladder disease but she died before they could effectively treat her. A doctor suggested that an autopsy be performed to determine the exact cause of death. The woman had three daughters, one of whom objected to the autopsy: "Why spend that kind of money? It won't bring Mom back."

The daughter's wishes were respected, however over the years as they aged and became ill with their own various ailments, they would undergo physical examinations. As part of taking their medical history, doctors routinely asked "And what was the cause of your mother's death?"

None could answer the question.

This is not a dramatic story. No mysterious genetic disorder ever occurred in any of her daughters, nor in any of their children. But each daughter (including the one who objected) at some point in her life, was confronted with the nagging question "What did Mom die of?"

AUTOPSIES PERFORMED BY MEDICAL EXAMINER

When a person dies, a physician must sign a medical certification stating the cause of death. This is not a problem if a person dies in a hospital or nursing home from natural causes. But if a person dies suddenly at home, for whatever reason, whoever discovers the body must call 911 to summon the police.

The police will ask the Medical Examiner to determine the cause of death in any of the following circumstances:
⇨ by poison, homicide, suicide, or accident
⇨ suddenly, when in apparent good health
⇨ when the decedent was not under the care of a physician
⇨ when death occurs in prison, or in police custody
⇨ in any unusual or suspicious circumstance
⇨ by disease posing a threat to public health
⇨ by disease, injury or toxic agent resulting from employment (FS 406.11).

The Medical Examiner will order an autopsy whenever he thinks it necessary to identify the cause of death. (FS 406.11). He will takes possession of the body. It will not be released until the examination is complete. In the interim, the family can proceed with arrangements for the funeral. The funeral director will contact the Medical Examiner to determine when he can pick up the body and proceed with the burial.

The cost of the autopsy is paid for by the county in which the body was found.

AUTOPSIES PERFORMED BY THE INSURANCE COMPANY

A company that issues health insurance in the state of Florida requires that the policy include a statement that the company has the right to perform an autopsy (FS 627.615). Most accident and life insurance policies contain similar provisions. The cost of the autopsy is paid for by the insurance company, so they will not order an autopsy unless there is some important reason to do so.

ANATOMICAL GIFTS

Hospital personnel determine whether a mortally ill patient is a candidate for an organ donation. Early on in the donor program those over 65 were not considered as suitable candidates. Today, however, the condition of the organ, and not the age, is the determining factor.

The federal government has established regional Organ Procurement Organizations throughout the United States to coordinate the donor program. There are four Organizations in Florida: LifeLink of Florida covering the West Coast, LifeQuest Organ Recovery Services for Northern Florida, TransLife/Florida Hospital covering the East Coast and Life Alliance covering Southern Florida. If it is decided that the patient is a candidate, the hospital will contact the local Organ Procurement Organizations. The Organization, together with the doctor who is treating the patient, will determine whether the patient is a suitable donor.

GIFT AUTHORIZED PRIOR TO DEATH

If, before death, the decedent made an anatomical gift by signing a donor card, then hospital personnel or the donor's doctor need to be made aware of the gift in quick proximity to the time of death — preferably before death. If it is determined that the donation is medically acceptable, the gift will be made. No family member need give permission, provided the hospital has a copy of the decedent's unrevoked donor card.

GIFT AUTHORIZED BY THE FAMILY

If no donor card is on record, and it is determined that the decedent is a suitable donor, someone who is specially trained will approach the family to request permission for the donation.

Florida statute states an order of priority for those who can give permission:

1st the person appointed by the decedent as his Health Care Surrogate

2nd spouse   3rd adult child

4th either parent   5th adult brother or sister

6th a grandparent

7th the court appointed Guardian, if any
(FS 765.512)

If permission is obtained from a family member and there are others in the same or a higher priority, then an effort must be made to contact those people and make them aware of the proposed gift. For example, if the mother of the candidate agrees to the gift (3rd in priority) and the decedent had adult children (2nd in priority), then the children must be made aware of the gift. If any one of the children objects, then no gift can be made.

The adult children of the decedent are second in priority to the spouse; however Florida Statute 765.512 creates an exception for the children — no gift can be made if the spouse agrees to an anatomical gift and one of the decedent's adult children objects. The statute also prohibits the donation if it is known that the decedent did not want to make such a gift or if the decedent would have objected to the donation based on his religious beliefs.

AFTER THE DONATION

Once the donation is made the body is delivered to the funeral home and prepared for burial or cremation as directed by the family. The donation does not disfigure the body so there can be an open casket viewing if the family so wishes.

Some regional Organ Procurement Organizations have an aftercare program that includes a letter of condolence to the family and an expression of gratitude for the gift. For privacy reasons, the identity of the recipient of the gift is not disclosed, but on request from the family, the local Organ Procurement Organization will give the family basic demographic information about the donation, such as the age, sex, marital status, number of children and occupation of the recipient of the gift.

GIFT FOR EDUCATION OR RESEARCH

Consider offering to release the body for the purpose of education or research in the event that the decedent signed a donor card, but was not an appropriate candidate for an organ donation. Not all offers are accepted. Most educational centers will not accept bodies from those who died from a contagious disease or from crushing injuries or who are extremely obese.

To get information about whether a donation will be accepted you need to call within 24 hours of the death. The ANATOMICAL BOARD OF THE STATE OF FLORIDA handles donations for the state. You can contact them at the University of Florida:

ANATOMICAL BOARD OF THE STATE OF FLORIDA
University of Florida, Health Science Center
P.O. Box 100235
Gainsville, FL 32610-0235
Telephone (800) 628-2594

Those who live in Miami can contact the University of Miami: University of Miami, School of Medicine
Department of Anatomy
P.O. Box 01690
Miami, FL 33101
Telephone (305) 547-6691

If the donation is accepted, you will need to coordinate the donation with the funeral director because the body will need a preliminary embalming procedure and then be transported to the university. There is no state subsidy for the program so the costs of transportation, preliminary embalming and final disposition of the body must be paid by the family. These costs may be significant, so if the donation was not specifically requested by the decedent, you need to ask the university about the cost of the donation before making the gift.

The study usually takes 18 months to 2 years. Once the study is complete the remains are cremated and the ashes placed in a cemetery that is local to the university; or if the family wishes, the *cremains* (cremated remains) will be returned to the family.

CAVEAT Federal law prohibits payment for organ donations (42 U.S.C. 274 e). There is no ban on payments made to prepare organs or tissue for transplantation nor is there any ban on charges made to transport bodies or body parts. Not-for-profit, as well as for-profit, companies have sprung up that are in the business of preparing and delivering body parts. These companies request donations from families — so they are not violating federal law by paying for the donation. The company prepares the body tissue or other parts of the donated body, and then distributes the parts throughout the United States to physicians, hospitals, research centers, etc. In many cases the monies charged for preparation and transportation includes a sizable profit.

If a company or organization other than your local Organ Procurement Organization approaches you to make a donation, before agreeing, you may want to learn about the company that is making the request.

What is the name of the company?

Where are their main headquarters located?

What is their primary business activity?

What is the name and job description of the person making the request?

DETERMINE THE END USE OF THE DONATION

You may want to ask what they intend to do with the tissue or body part. If it is being used for research, then what type of research? Where is the research being conducted? If it will be used for transplantation, then what agency (doctor, hospital) will receive the donation and where is that agency located?

Once you have this information you can make an informed decision as to whether you wish to make the donation to that organization.

THE FUNERAL

Approximately ten percent of deaths occur suddenly because of accident, suicide, foul play or undetected illness. But, in general, death occurs after a lengthy illness, with a common scenario being that of an aged person who dies after being ill for several months, if not years. In such case, family and friends are emotionally prepared for the happening. Expected or not, the first job is the disposition of the body.

THE PREARRANGED FUNERAL

Increasingly, people are arranging, in advance, for their own funeral and burial. This makes it easier on the family both financially and emotionally. All the decisions have been made and there is no guessing what the decedent would have wanted.

If the decedent made provision for his burial, you should come across a burial certificate, or perhaps a deed to a burial space. If he made provision for his funeral, you should find a Preneed Funeral Contract or a Burial Agreement. You need to read the Agreement to determine what provisions were made. If the Agreement was paid by installments, you need to determine whether it is paid in full. You also need to determine whether the contract was a fixed price agreement or whether there will be additional charges.

If you cannot locate the Agreement, but you know the decedent made provision for his burial and funeral, then call the funeral home and ask them to send you a copy of the contract. If you believe the decedent purchased a funeral plan but you do not know the name of the funeral home, call the local funeral homes. Many funeral homes are owned by national firms with computer capacity to identify people who have purchased a contract at any of their many locations.

Once you have possession of the Agreement, take it with you to the funeral home and go over the terms of the Agreement with the funeral director. Inquire whether there will be any charge that is not included in the contract.

MAKING FUNERAL ARRANGEMENTS

If the decedent died unexpectedly or without having made any prior funeral arrangements, your first job is to choose a funeral director and make arrangements for the funeral or cremation. Most people choose the nearest or most conveniently located funeral home without   comparison shopping. However prices for these services can vary significantly from funeral home to funeral home. Savings can be had if you take the time to make a few phone calls.

Receiving price quotes by telephone is your right under both state and federal law (Federal Trade Commission ("FTC") Rule 453.2 (b) (1), FS 470.034). The funeral director is required to give an accurate telephone quote of the prices of his goods and services. Funeral homes are listed in the telephone directory under FUNERAL DIRECTORS. If you live in a small town, there may be only one or two listings. If such is the case, then check out some funeral homes in the next largest city.

Funeral directors usually provide the following services:
- ➢ arrange for the transportation of the body
    to the funeral home and then to the burial site
- ➢ obtain burial transit permits
- ➢ arrange for the embalming or cremation of the body
- ➢ arrange funeral and memorial services
    and the viewing of the body
- ➢ obtain information for the death certificate
- ➢ order copies of the death certificate for the family
- ➢ have memorial cards printed.

To compare prices you will need to determine:

✧ what is included in the price of a basic funeral plan

✧ whether you can expect any additional cost.

If the decedent did not own a burial space, that cost must be included when making funeral arrangements. Embalming is necessary if you are going to have a viewing. Embalming is not necessary if you order a direct cremation or an immediate burial. Both state and federal law prohibit any charge for embalming, or any other service, unless you order that service (FS 470.035, FTC Rule 453.5).

PURCHASING THE CASKET

When comparison-shopping, you will find that the single most expensive item in the funeral arrangement is the casket. Most funeral directors will quote you a price for a basic funeral plan that does not include the cost of the casket. Directors usually quote a range of prices for the casket, saying that you will need to come in and choose the casket at the time you contract for the funeral.

When selecting a casket you need to be aware that there may be a considerable mark-up in the price quoted by the funeral director. You do not need to go "sole source" when purchasing the casket. You can purchase the casket elsewhere and have it delivered to the funeral home to be used instead of the one offered by the funeral director. Funeral homes are required to accept caskets purchased elsewhere, and they may not charge a handling fee for accepting that casket. But if the price list given to you by the funeral home states that the price of their casket includes a specific dollar amount for basic services, then the funeral director is allowed to add that dollar amount to the charge for his services, should you purchase the casket elsewhere (FTC Rule 453.2, 453.4).

Caskets are not usually displayed for sale in a shopping mall, so most of us have no idea of the going price for a casket. With the advent of the Internet, you can learn all about the cost of any item, even a casket, by using your search engine to find a retail casket sales dealer. If you are not computer literate, you can locate the nearest retail casket sales outlet by looking in the yellow pages under CASKETS. You may need to look in the telephone directory for the nearest large city to find a listing. By making a call to a retail casket sales dealer, you will become knowledgeable in the price range of caskets. You can then decide what is a reasonable price for the product you seek.

The best time to do your comparison shopping is before you go to the funeral home to arrange for the funeral. Once you have determined what you should pay for the casket, it is only fair to give the funeral director the opportunity to meet that price. If you cannot reach a meeting of the minds, you can always order the casket from the retail sales dealer and have it delivered to the funeral home.

ON-LINE FUNERAL SERVICES

The Internet is changing the way the world does business, and the funeral industry is no exception. A growing number of mortuaries are offering live Webcasts of funerals and wakes for those who are unable to pay their respects in person.

There are Web sites where you can post an obituary. There are on-line memorial chat rooms as well as on-line eulogies and testimonials. There is even a Web site that offers a posthumous e-mail service which allows people to leave final messages for friends and relatives. You can locate these services using your favorite search engine and typing in "obituaries."

THE CREMATION

Increasingly people are opting for cremation. Based on statistics published by the **CREMATION ASSOCIATION OF NORTH AMERICA**, approximately half of those who die each year in Florida are cremated. That percentage is growing. The reasons for choosing cremation are varied, but for the majority, it is a matter of finances. The cost of cremation is approximately one-sixth that of an ordinary funeral and burial. A major saving is the cost of the casket. No casket is necessary for the cremation and Federal law prohibits a Funeral Director from saying that a casket is required for a direct cremation (FTC Rule 453.3 (b)ii). You may need a suitable container to deliver the body to the crematory. After the cremation, you will need an urn for the ashes.

If you are having a memorial service in a place of worship and no viewing of the body before the cremation, then consider contracting with a facility that does cremations only. Look in the telephone book under **CREMATION SERVICES**. You will also see cremation "societies" in the telephone book. Some are for-profit and others non-profit. You can also find advertisements for cremation services on the Internet. These cremation facilities provide much the same services as a funeral home but with one important exception — the cremation service does not provide any type of funeral service or public viewing of the body.

THE OVERWEIGHT DECEDENT

If the decedent weighs more than 300 pounds, then you need to check to see if the cremation service has facilities large enough to handle the body. You will need to make burial arrangements if you cannot locate a crematory that can accommodate the body.

THE DECEDENT WITH A PACEMAKER

Cremating a body with a pacemaker or any radiation producing device can cause damage to the cremation chamber or to the person performing the cremation. If the decedent was wearing such electronic aid, then you need to investigate the cost of having it removed prior to the cremation. Some Veterinarian hospitals are implanting used pacemakers into pets who are suffering from heart disease. You might consider asking a Veterinarian to remove the pacemaker in exchange for a donation of the pacemaker to the hospital.

DISPOSING OF THE ASHES

You will need a suitable urn for burial, if the cremains are to be placed in a cemetery. You can purchase the urn from the funeral director or Crematory Service Director. Urns cost much less than caskets, but they can cost several hundred dollars. You may wish to do some comparison shopping by calling a retail sales casket dealer.

Many cemeteries have a separate building called a *columbarium* which is especially designed to store urns. Some cemeteries allow the cremains of a family member to be placed in an occupied family plot or mausoleum If you wish to have the cremains placed in an occupied mausoleum or family plot, you need to call the cemetery and ask them to explain their policy as it relates to the burial of urns in occupied spaces.

SCATTERED AT SEA

The decedent may have expressed a desire to have his ashes placed at sea. The funeral director or cremation director should be able to assist you in seeing to it that these wishes are respected. Federal law prohibits the ashes from being scattered any closer than three nautical miles from land, so you will need to arrange to have a boat carry the ashes out to sea (Title 40 Code of Federal Regulations ("CFR") Section 229.1).

BURIAL AT SEA

Burying a body at sea is more complicated than scattering ashes at sea. Under Florida law, permission from the Medical Examiner must be obtained before the decedent can be buried at sea (FS 406.11). Again, the funeral director should be able to assist with the arrangements for burial.

THE OUT OF STATE BURIAL

If the decedent is to be buried in another state, then the body will need to be transported to that state. Many states, including Florida, require a Burial-Transit Permit for the burial or for removal of the body from the state where the death occurred (FS 382.006). If services are to be held in Florida and in another state, contact a local funeral director and he will make arrangements with the out of state funeral home for the transportation of the body.

If you do not plan to have services conducted in Florida, you can contact the out-of-state funeral director and ask him to effect the transfer. Many funeral homes belong to a national network of funeral homes, so both the local and the out-of-state funeral director usually have the means to make arrangements to transport the body.

TRANSPORTING CREMAINS
If the body has been cremated, you can transport the cremains yourself, either by carrying the ashes as part of your luggage or by arranging with the airline to transport the ashes as cargo. Have a certified copy of the death certificate and the Burial-Transit Permit ready in the event that you need to identify the cremains of the decedent.

In these days of heightened security, it is important to call the airline before departure and ask whether they have any special regulation or procedure regarding the transportation of human ashes.

SPOUSE ▶ THE MILITARY BURIAL

Subject to availability of burial spaces, an honorably discharged veteran and/or his unmarried minor or handicapped child and/or his unremarried spouse may be buried in a national military cemetery. Some cemeteries have room only for cremated remains or for the casketed remains of a family member of someone who is currently buried in that cemetery.

In Florida, the St. Augustine National Cemetery has no space available, but there are three other national cemeteries that have spaces available at this time:

Barrancas National Cemetery;
Naval Air Station
Pensacola, FL   32408-1099
Telephone (850) 452-3357

Bay Pines National Cemetery
P.O. Box 477
Bay Pines, FL   33504-0477
Telephone (352) 793-7740

Florida National Cemetery
6592 SW 102nd Avenue
Bushnell, FL 33513
Telephone (352) 793-1074

An honorably discharged veteran can be buried in the national military cemetery at Arlington, Virginia. The Department of the Army is in charge of the Arlington National Cemetery. You can call them at (703) 695-3250 for information about having a veteran buried there.

THE COST OF A
MILITARY BURIAL

Burial space in a National Cemetery is free of charge. Cemetery employees will open and close the grave and mark it with a headstone or grave marker without cost to the family. If requested, the local Veteran's Administration ("VA") will provide the family with a memorial flag. The VA will not pay to have the body transported to the cemetery, so the family needs to make arrangements with a funeral firm to transport the remains to the cemetery.

Regardless of where an honorably discharged veteran is buried, allowances may be available for the plot, and the burial and grave marker expenses. The amount varies depending on factors such as whether the veteran died because of a service related injury. The VA will not reimburse any burial or funeral expense for the spouse of a veteran. For information about reimbursement of funeral and burial expenses you can call the VA at (800) 827-1000.

The Department of Veteran's Affairs has a Web site with information on the following topics:

> ➤ National and Military Cemeteries
> ➤ Burial, Headstones and Markers
> ➤ State Cemetery Grants Program
> ➤ Obtaining Military Records
> ➤ Locating Veterans

 VA CEMETERY WEB SITE
http://www.cem.va.gov

BENEFITS FOR SPOUSE OF DECEASED VETERAN

| SPOUSE |

The surviving spouse of an honorably discharged veteran should contact the Veteran's Administration to determine whether he/she is eligible for any benefits. For example, if the decedent had minor or disabled children, his spouse may also be eligible for a monthly benefit of Dependency and Indemnity Compensation ("DIC"). If the Veteran's surviving spouse receives nursing home care under Medicaid, he/she might be eligible for monthly payments from the VA.

Whether a surviving spouse is eligible for any of these benefits depends on many factors including whether the decedent was serving on active duty, whether his death was service related, and the surviving spouse's assets and income. DIC benefits are discontinued should the surviving spouse remarry; however, the law allows payments to be resumed in the event the subsequent marriage ends because of death or divorce.

For information about whether the surviving spouse is eligible for any benefit related to the decedent's military service call the VA at (800) 827-1000. You can receive a printed statement of public policy: VA Pamphlet 051-000-00217-2 FEDERAL BENEFITS FOR VETERANS AND DEPENDENTS by sending a check in the amount of $5 to

THE SUPERINTENDENT OF DOCUMENTS
P.O. Box 371954
Pittsburgh, PA 15250-7954

Information is also available at the VA Web site.

 VETERAN'S ADMINISTRATION
http://www.va.gov

 **LAWYER**   ## THE WRONGFUL DEATH

When a death is cause by the wrongful or negligent act of another, the person appointed by the Court to settle the decedent's Estate may sue on behalf of anyone who is entitled to be compensated for the loss. Monies that can be recovered for a **wrongful death** are regulated by Florida Statute 768.21:

THE DECEDENT'S ESTATE: Medical and funeral expenses due to the decedent's injury or death.

DEPENDENT: Anyone who was dependent upon the decedent can be awarded money for lost support.

SPOUSE and MINOR CHILD: The decedent's spouse and minor children may recover for lost support, loss of companionship, and pain and suffering.

PARENT: The parent of a minor child can be awarded money for mental pain and suffering from the date of the injury. The parent of an adult child is entitled to recover for pain and suffering, provided the deceased child had no other survivors; i.e., spouse, child or dependent relative.

The astute reader (one who is probably an attorney) will notice that there is someone missing from this list, namely the decedent's adult child. In an effort to reduce the amount of large awards suffered by the medical industry, the Florida legislature limited the *damages* (amount that could be awarded) and potential *plaintiffs* (people who have a right to sue).

Under Florida statute 768.21, if a death was caused by the wrongful or negligent act of another, the decedent's survivors are entitled to lost support, medical and funeral expenses; but these awards are relatively small. Large awards result from losses suffered for lost companionship and pain and suffering. Under this law, relatives eligible for such compensation are limited to spouse, minor child, parent of a minor child and parent of an adult child who has no other survivors.

Florida has a large senior citizen population. If the wrongful death of an elderly person was caused by the malpractice of a doctor, nurse, hospital, nursing home, etc., there can be no award for such losses unless there is a surviving spouse. The adult child of a single parent cannot sue for loss of companionship or pain and suffering, no matter how wrongfully or negligently the medical community behaved. Hopefully, people will prevail upon their legislators to change this law.

 **LAWYER**   THE ACCIDENTAL DEATH

It is important to have a Personal Injury attorney investigate any accidental death, to determine whether the death was caused by the wrongful act of a person, or company. If the accident was related to the decedent's job, the family may wish to consult with a Worker's Compensation attorney as well.

The State of Florida reimburses crime victims and/or their dependents, who suffer loses that are not covered by insurance, public funds or any other compensation. If the decedent died because of a criminal act, you may be eligible to be reimbursed for loses under the Florida **VICTIM ASSISTANCE ACT.** Compensation can be awarded for funeral and burial expenses, for medical expenses, psychological counseling, lost support, lost wages, etc.

The Office of Attorney General administers the program. To be eligible, the following must be true:

➤ The decedent was an innocent victim.

➤ The crime was reported to authorities within five days of the discovery of the body.

➤ There was full cooperation with law enforcement officers by the victim and/or his family.

➤ Application for compensation was filed within one year from the commission of the crime or discovery of the body (FS 960.13).

Awards are based on an "actual need" basis. Total compensation may not exceed $25,000.
To file a claim you can call (800) 226-6667 or write:
**Bureau of Victim Compensation
The Capitol, PL-01
Tallahassee, FL 32399-1050**
You can download a Crime Victim Compensation Application from the Attorney General's Web site.

**OFFICE OF ATTORNEY GENERAL
http://myfloridalegal.com**

When an inmate of any state, county or municipal institution dies, the superintendent, or other person in charge, will notify the relative of the decedent. If no relative can be found, or if no one will take responsibility for the disposition of the body, the person in charge of the body will offer it to the Anatomical Board of the State of Florida for the purpose of education or research.

The same procedure is followed in the case of an indigent or unclaimed body. Police make every effort to identify and locate the family of an unclaimed body. If no one is willing to claim the body, it is offered to the Anatomical Board. If the body is not suitable for study, or if they do not need the body, the Anatomical Board will notify the Department of Health that the donation is declined. Upon such notification, the Department of Health will arrange for burial at public expense (FS 406.53).

THE INDIGENT VETERAN

Honorably discharged veterans who are indigent, can be buried without charge as described on page 18. Whoever is in charge of the veteran's burial will not offer the body to the Anatomical Board, unless the decedent expressed a desire to do so.

Special Situation

THE PROBLEM FUNERAL OR BURIAL

The funeral and burial industry is well regulated by the state and federal government. In Florida, the following acts are subject to disciplinary action:

⊠ Using intimidation or pressure to sell services

⊠ Using a false or misleading advertisement

⊠ Paying kick-backs

⊠ Taking possession of a dead body without first getting permission from an authorized person

⊠ requiring a casket to be purchased for cremation (FS 470.036).

Funeral directors are licensed professionals so it is unusual to have a problem with the funeral or burial or cremation. If, however, you had a bad experience with any aspect of the funeral or disposition of the body, you can file a complaint with the Office of the Comptroller, Investigative Division of the Department of Financial Services at (800) 323-2627.

 **LAWYER**

In addition to filing a complaint with the Board, you may wish to consult with an attorney who is experienced in litigation matters to learn of any other legal remedy that you may have.

 **LAWYER**   THE MISSING BODY

Few things are more difficult to deal with than a missing person. The emotional turmoil created by the "not knowing" is often more difficult than the finality of death. The legal problems created by the disappearance are also more difficult than if the person simply died. It may take a two-part legal process — the appointment of a Conservator to handle the missing person's affairs while he is missing, and the Probate proceeding after the Probate Court has issued an order that the missing person is presumed to be dead.

APPOINTING A CONSERVATOR

An ***Absentee*** is a person who is missing and cannot be found after a diligent search. If the Absentee has business matters that need attending (bills that need to be paid, family to be supported), his next of kin can ask the Probate Court to appoint a Conservator of the Absentee's property (FL 747.02). The Conservator will manage the property, under Court supervision, until the person can be found. You will need an attorney, experienced in Probate matters, to have the Conservator appointed.

BEGINNING THE PROBATE PROCEDURE

Anyone who has the right to inherit the Absentee's property can begin the Probate process any time there is sufficient evidence that the Absentee is dead, or after the Absentee has been missing for five years. The Judge will hear evidence to determine whether the missing person should be presumed dead; and if so, the Probate proceeding can go forward (FL 731.103),

THE DEATH CERTIFICATE

It is the job of the funeral director to provide information about the decedent to the State Registrar. The Office of Vital Statistics will prepare a death certificate based on that information. It is important that the information you give to the funeral or cremation director is correct. You need to check the form completed by the funeral director to be sure names are correctly spelled and dates correctly written. Once the information is sent to Vital Statistics, it will be difficult and time consuming to make a correction.

The funeral director will order as many certified copies of the death certificate as you request. Most establishments require an original certified copy and not a photocopy so you need to order sufficient certified copies. The following is a list of institutions that may request a certified copy:

* Each insurance company that insured the decedent or his property (health insurance, life insurance, car insurance, etc.)
* Each financial institution in which the decedent had money invested (brokerage houses, banks)
* The decedent's pension fund
* Each credit card company used by the decedent
* The IRS
* The Social Security Administration
* The Motor Vehicle department
* If a Probate proceeding is necessary, then the Clerk of the Probate Court.

Some airlines and car rental companies offer a discount for short notice, emergency trips. If you have family flying in for the funeral, you may wish to order a few extra copies of the death certificate so that they can obtain an airline or car rental discount.

CLERK REQUIRES CERTIFICATE WITHOUT CAUSE OF DEATH

Florida statute 382.008 (6) requires state agencies to keep confidential information relating to the cause of a person's death, so the Clerk will record only those death certificates issued in Florida that do NOT state the cause of death. As discussed previously, the funeral director will obtain death certificates for you, both with and without, the cause of death. Forward a certified copy of the death certificate that does not state the cause of death to the Clerk.

If the decedent died in another state, that state may issue only one type of certificate — one that states the cause of death. If the decedent died in another state, then, respecting the law of that state, the Clerk will record a certified copy of the out-of-state death certificate, even though the certificate may disclose the cause of death.

Of course, you are free to order a copy of the death certificate that states the cause of death for your own personal records.

If you wish to order certified copies of the death certificate at a later date, you can call the funeral director and ask him to do so or you can write to:

OFFICE OF VITAL STATISTICS
Attn: Customer Services
P.O. Box 210
Jacksonville, FL   32231-0042

You may wish to first call at (904) 359-6900 Extension 1029 and ask them what information they require and the cost of obtaining a certified copy. Also ask how long it will take to receive your copy and the cost of obtaining a copy quickly.

VIA THE INTERNET
You can download the death certificate order form from the Internet.

 FLORIDA DEPARTMENT OF HEALTH
http://www.doh.state.fl.us

WALK-IN
You can obtain a certified copy of the death certificate from the Office of Vital Statistics in Jacksonville:

Office of Vital Statistics
1217 Pearl Street
Jacksonville, FL 32202

Lobby hours are 8:30 a.m. to 4:30 p.m.

ABOUT PROBATE

Once a person dies, all of the property he owns as of the date of his death is referred to as the *decedent's Estate.* If the decedent owned property that was in his name only (not jointly or in trust for someone) then some sort of Court procedure may be necessary to determine who is entitled to possession of the property. The name of the Court procedure is *Probate*.

We will use the term "Court" or "Probate Court" to refer to the judge who is presiding over Probate matters.

The root of the word Probate is "to prove." It refers to the first job of the Probate Court, that is, to examine proof of whether the decedent left a valid Will. The second job of the Probate Court is to appoint someone to wrap up the affairs of the decedent by paying the cost of the Probate procedure, any outstanding bills, and then distributing whatever is left to the proper beneficiary. If the decedent left a valid Will naming someone as *Executor* of his Estate, the Court will appoint that person for the job and issue *Letters Testamentary* giving him authority to administer the Estate. If the decedent died without a Will, the Court will appoint someone to be the *Administrator* of his Estate and issue *Letters of Administration.*

For simplicity we will refer to the person appointed by the Court to settle the decedent's Estate as the **Personal Representative**, and the document authorizing him to act, as **Letters**.

There are different ways to conduct a Probate procedure depending on the value of the property that is being Probated, and whether the decedent owned real property at the time of his death. We will refer to the property that is distributed as part of a Probate proceeding as the decedent's **Probate Estate** and the method of conducting the Probate, as the **Estate Administration**.

Chapter 6 explains the different kinds of Estate Administration \that are available in the state of Florida.

But we are getting ahead of ourselves. First we need to determine whether Probate is necessary. To answer that question we need to know exactly what the decedent owned, so the next two chapters explain how to identify, and then locate, all of the decedent's assets.

Giving Notice Of The Death 2

Those closest to the decedent usually notify family members and close friends by telephone. The funeral director will arrange to have an obituary published in as many different newspapers as the family requests, but there is still the job of notifying the government and people who were doing business with the decedent. That job is the duty of whoever is appointed as Personal Representative of the decedent's Estate.

Florida law gives an order of priority for the appointment of Personal Representative. Whoever the decedent named as Executor or Personal Representative of his Will has top priority. Once appointed, it is his job to give notice of the death. If the decedent died *intestate*, i.e. without a Will, the decedent's spouse has priority to be appointed as Personal Representative, so the surviving spouse to let every one know of the death (FL 733.301). If there is no spouse, the job falls to his next of kin. By *next of kin,* we mean those people who inherit the decedent's property according to Florida's RULES GOVERNING INTESTATE SUCCESSION. Those laws are explained in Chapter 5.

The person who has the job of settling the decedent's Estate should begin to give notice as soon as is practicable after the death. Two government agencies that need to be notified are the Social Security Administration and the IRS. This chapter gives their telephone number as well as those of all the other agencies that need to be notified.

NOTIFYING SOCIAL SECURITY

Many funeral directors will, as part of their service package, notify the Social Security Administration of the death. You may wish to check to see that this has been done. You can do so by calling (800) 772-1213. If you are hearing impaired, call (800) 325-0778 TTY. You will need to give the Social Security Administration the full legal name of the decedent as well as his social security number and date of birth.

 **DECEDENT RECEIVING SOCIAL SECURITY**

If the decedent was receiving checks from Social Security, you need to determine whether his last check needs to be returned to the Social Security Administration. Each Social Security check is a payment for the prior month, provided that person lives for the entire prior month. If the decedent died on the last day of the month, you should not cash the check for that month.

For example, if he died on July 31st, you need to return the check that Social Security mails out in August. If however, he died August 1st, the check sent in August need not be returned because that check is payment for the month of July.

If the Social Security check is electronically deposited into a bank account, notify the bank and the Social Security Administration that the account holder died. If the check needs to be returned, the Social Security Administration will withdraw it electronically from the bank account. You will need to keep the account open until the funds are withdrawn.

SPOUSE/CHILD'S SOCIAL SECURITY BENEFITS

SPOUSE

If the decedent had sufficient work credits, the Social Security Administration will give the decedent's widow(er), or if unmarried, then the decedent's minor children, a one-time death benefit in the amount of $255.

SURVIVORS BENEFITS

The spouse (or former spouse) of the decedent may be eligible for Survivors Benefits. Benefits vary depending on the amount of work credits earned by the decedent; whether the decedent had minor or disabled children; the spouse's age; how long they were married, etc. The minor child of the decedent may be eligible for benefits regardless of whether the child's father (the decedent) ever married the child's mother. Paternity can be established by any one of several methods including the father acknowledging his child in writing or verbally to members of his family. For more information you can call the Social Security Administration at (800) 772-1213.

SOCIAL SECURITY BENEFITS

A spouse or former spouse can collect social security benefits based on the decedent's work record. This value may be greater than the spouse now receives. It is important to make an appointment with your local Social Security office and determine whether you as the spouse (or former spouse) or parent of decedent's minor child are eligible for any Social Security or Survivor benefit. You can down load publications that explain survivors benefits from the Social Security Web site.

SOCIAL SECURITY ADMINISTRATION
http://www.ssa.gov

DECEDENT WITH GOVERNMENT PENSION

Any pension or annuity check received after the date of death of a federal retiree, or a survivor annuitant, needs to be returned to the U.S. Treasury. If the check is direct deposited to a bank account, call the financial institution and ask them to return the check. If the check is sent by mail, you need to return it to the return mail address on the Department of Treasury envelope in which the check was mailed. Include a letter explaining the reason for the return of the check and stating the decedent's date of death.

$$$ APPLY FOR BENEFITS $$$

A survivor annuity may be available to a surviving spouse, and/or minor or disabled child. In some cases, a former spouse may be eligible for benefits. Even though you notify the government of the death, they will not automatically give you benefits to which you may be entitled. You need to apply for those benefits by notifying the Office of Personnel Management ("OPM") of the death and requesting that they send you an application for survivor benefits. You can call them at (888) 767-6738 or you can write to:

U. S. OFFICE OF PERSONNEL MANAGEMENT
RETIREMENT OPERATIONS CENTER
Post Office Box 45
Boyers, PA 16017-4500

You will find brochures and information about Survivor's Benefits at the OPM Web site.

 U.S. OFFICE OF PERSONNEL MANAGEMENT
http://www.opm.gov

DECEDENT WITH COMPANY PENSION OR ANNUITY

In most cases, pension and annuity checks are payment for the prior month. If the decedent received his pension or annuity check before his death, then no monies need be returned. Pension checks and/or annuity checks received after the date of death may need to be returned to the company. You need to notify the company of the death to determine the status of the last check sent to the decedent.

Before notifying the company, locate the policy or pension statement that is the basis of the income. That document should tell whether there is a beneficiary of the pension or annuity funds now that the pensioner or annuitant is dead. If you cannot locate the document, use the return address on the check envelope and ask the company to send you a copy of the plan. Also request that they forward to you any claim form that may be required in order for the survivor or beneficiary to receive benefits under that pension plan or policy.

If the pension/annuity check is direct deposited to the decedent's account, ask the bank to assist you in locating the company and notifying the company of the death.

Anyone who is a beneficiary of an Individual Retirement Account ("IRA") or QRP needs to keep in mind that income taxes may not have been paid on monies placed in an IRA or QRP account. In such case, significant taxes may be due when the money is withdrawn. You need to learn what options are available to you as a beneficiary of the plan and the tax consequences of each option. You will need to ask an accountant how much will be due in taxes for each option. Once you know all the facts, you will be able to make the best choice for your circumstance.

 **SPOUSE** There are special options available if the spouse is the beneficiary of the decedent's IRA account. The spouse has the right to withdraw the money from the account or roll it over into the spouse's own retirement account. Although the employer can explain options that are available, the spouse still needs to understand the tax consequence of choosing any given option. It is important to consult with an accountant to determine the best way to go.

If the decedent had a QRP, the plan may permit the spouse to roll the balance of the account into a new IRA. The spouse needs to contact the decedent's employer for an explanation of the plan and all the options that are available at this time.

NOTIFYING IRS

THE FINAL INCOME TAX RETURN
The surviving spouse can file a final joint income tax return. If there is no surviving spouse, it is the Personal Representative's job to file the decedent's final return. If no Probate proceeding is necessary, whoever takes possession of the decedent's property needs to file the final return.

The decedent's final federal income tax return (IRS form 1040) needs to be filed by April 15th of the year following the year in which he died. You can get information about filing the final income tax return by calling the Internal Revenue Service at (800) 829-3676, or you can visit their Web site.

 INTERNAL REVENUE SERVICES
http://www.irs.gov

You may want to keep the decedent's bank account open until you determine whether the decedent is entitled to an income tax refund. See Chapter 6 for an explanation of how to obtain a tax refund.

THE GOOD NEWS
Monies inherited from the decedent are generally not counted as income to you, so you do not pay federal income tax on those monies. If the monies you inherit later earn interest or income for you, then of course you will report that income as you do any other type of income.

AN ESTATE TAX FOR THE WEALTHY

Both the federal and state government have the right to impose an *Estate Tax* on property transferred to a beneficiary as a result of the death. All the property owned as of the date of death becomes the decedent's *Taxable Estate.* This includes *real property* (residential lots, condominiums etc.) and *personal property* (life insurance policies, cars, business interests, securities, IRA accounts, etc.). It includes property held in the decedent's name alone, as well as property that he held jointly or in Trust. It also includes gifts given by the decedent during his lifetime that exceeded $10,000 per person, per year. In the year 2002, the *Annual Gift Tax Exclusion* was adjusted for inflation to $11,000 (26 U.S.C. 2503).

For most of us, this is not a concern because no federal Estate Tax need be paid unless the decedent's Taxable Estate exceeds the federal *Estate Tax Exclusion* amount. That value is currently one and a half million dollars and is scheduled to go even higher:

YEAR	ESTATE TAX EXCLUSION AMOUNT
2005	$1,500,000
2006-2008	$2,000,000
2009	$3,500,000

In 2010 the federal Estate Tax is scheduled to be phased out altogether; however in 2011, the Estate Tax will be reinstated with an Exclusion Amount of $1,000,000, unless lawmakers change the law again.

There is an unlimited marital tax deduction for property transferred to the surviving spouse; so in most cases, no Estate tax need be paid if the decedent was married. Regardless of whether taxes are due, federal and state Estate tax returns must be filed whenever the decedent's Estate exceeds the federal Estate Tax Exclusion Amount in effect as of his date of death. Both state and federal return are due within 9 months of the date of death (FS 198.13).

THE FLORIDA "PICK-UP" TAX

The Florida Estate tax is based on the federal Estate Tax. The federal government imposes a tax on all property transferred because of the death. The federal government then grants an Estate Tax credit, so that no tax need be paid unless the amount transferred is more than a given dollar value. That dollar value is the federal Estate Tax Exclusion Amount (see prior page). The Florida Estate Tax is called a "pick-up" tax, because the state collects the tax that would have gone to the federal government had it not been for the federal Estate Tax credit.

As with the federal Estate Tax, no tax need be paid to the state of Florida, unless the decedent's Taxable Estate exceeds the current federal Tax Exclusion amount. But for those Estates that are larger than the Exclusion Amount, Estate Taxes will need to be paid to the federal government and to the state of Florida. And that includes property transferred within Florida regardless of whether the decedent was a resident of the state (FS 198.02).

As explained, the federal Estate Tax is scheduled to be phased out and then reinstated in 2011. The Florida Estate Tax is based on the federal Estate Tax credit, so unless the legislature changes things, the Florida Estate Tax will go the way of the federal Estate Tax.

Both state and federal government do not tax property passing to the decedent's spouse, however, once the surviving spouse dies, all of his Estate is subject to Estate taxes. As we will see in Chapter 7, setting up a Revocable Living Trust can significantly reduce the amount of federal and Florida Estate Taxes that may need to be paid once the surviving spouse dies.

THE UN-UNIFIED GIFT TAX

Up until the year 2002, if you gave someone more than $10,000 in any given year you had to report that gift to the IRS. As explained, the Annual Gift Tax Exclusion is now adjusted for the cost of living and is currently $11,000. The IRS keeps a running count of amounts that you give over the Annual Gift Tax Exclusion each year. Although you are required to report the gift, no tax need be paid unless that running total is more than the federal Estate Tax Exclusion amount. If your running total does not exceed that amount during your lifetime, once you die, the cumulative value of gifts reported to the IRS will be added to your Taxable Estate.

Until the tax law was changed, the Gift and Estate Tax were unified. No Gift Tax needed to be paid unless the total value of the taxable gifts exceeded the federal Estate Tax Exclusion amount. In 2004 that changed. The Estate Tax Exclusion amount went up to $1,500,000, but the amount for the Gift Tax Exclusion remained at $1,000,000, so they now are no longer unified.

To summarize:
If you make a gift to anyone that is greater than the Annual Gift Tax Exclusion for that year, you must report the gift to the IRS. The IRS will keep count of values that you gave in excess of the Annual Gift Tax Exclusion. In 2004, and thereafter, if that sum exceeds $1,000,000, you will pay a Gift Tax on any amount that you give that is over the Annual Gift Tax Exclusion.

The Estate Tax is scheduled to be repealed in 2010, but not the Gift Tax.

Florida does not have a Gift Tax at this time.

The current federal Estate Tax is scheduled to be phased out in the year 2010, but a new Capital Gains Tax is scheduled for 2010 that may prove even more costly than the Estate Tax. The new Capital Gains Tax is related to the way inherited property is evaluated by the federal government. Real and personal property is inherited at a "step up" in basis, meaning that if the decedent's property has increased in value from the time he acquired it, the beneficiary will inherit the property at its fair market value as of the decedent's date of death. For example, if the decedent bought stock for $20,000 and it is worth $50,000 as of his date of death, the beneficiary will take a step-up in basis of $30,000; i.e. the beneficiary inherits the stock at the current $50,000 value. If the beneficiary sells the stock for $50,000, he pays no Capital Gains Tax. If the beneficiary holds onto the stock and later sells it for $60,000, the beneficiary will pay a Capital Gains Tax only on the $10,000 increase in value since the decedent's death.

Up to 2009, there is no limit to the amount a beneficiary can take as a step-up in basis. But in 2010 caps are set in place. The decedent's Estate will be allowed a 1.3 million dollar step-up in basis, plus another 3 million for property passing to the surviving spouse. The new law could result in significant Capital Gains Taxes that the beneficiary must pay. For example, suppose in 2010 you inherit a business from your father that he purchased for $100,000 and it is now worth 2 million dollars. There is a capital gain of 1.9 million dollars, but you are allowed a step-up in basis of only 1.3 million. If you sell it for 2 million dollars $600,000 of your inheritance will be subject to a Capital Gains Tax.

SPOUSE ▸ SELLING THE HOME

In the tough "ole days" the IRS used to allow Capital Gains Tax Exclusion (up to $125,000) on the sale of one's **homestead** (the principal residence). A person had to be 55 or older to take advantage of the Exclusion, and it was a once-in-a-lifetime tax break. If a married couple sold their home and took the Tax Exclusion it was "used up" and no longer available to either partner.

In these, the good times, the IRS allows you to sell your home and up to $250,000 ($500,000 for a married couple) of the profit is free of the Capital Gains Tax. There is no limit to the number of times you can use the Exclusion, provided you own and live in the home at least two of the last five years prior to the sale (26 U.S.C. 121).

If, under the old law, the decedent and his spouse used their "once in a lifetime" Homestead Tax Exclusion, with this new law, the surviving spouse can sell the homestead and once again take advantage of a tax break.

People who own a residence in Florida are entitled to a Homestead Tax Exemption of up to $25,000 of the assessed tax valuation. If the decedent's homestead is transferred through sale or inheritance, the county Property Appraiser must be notified of the change of ownership. If the new owner does not occupy the property as his Florida homestead, he needs to notify the county Property Appraiser that the property is no longer homestead property.

A new owner who occupies the property as his primary and permanent home needs to apply to the county Property Appraiser for his own Homestead Tax Exemption on before January 1st in order to receive the Exemption for the taxable year. Tax Exemptions are also available for those who are widowed or who are permanently disabled (FS 196.031, 196.101, 196.202).

You can get information about property taxes including the telephone number and address of the Property Appraiser in your county from the Internet.

FLORIDA DEPARTMENT OF REVENUE
http://www.state.fl.us/dor

DECEDENT WITH A TRUST

A decedent who was the **Grantor** (or *Settlor*) of a Trust, was probably managing the Trust as *Trustee* during his lifetime. The document that sets out the terms of the Trust (the **Trust Agreement)** should name a **Successor Trustee** to manage the Trust now that the Grantor is deceased. The Agreement may instruct the Successor Trustee to make certain gifts once the Grantor dies or the Trust document may direct the Successor Trustee to hold money in trust for a beneficiary of the Trust.

 **☎ LAWYER**   IF YOU ARE
SUCCESSOR TRUSTEE

If you are the Successor Trustee, then in addition to following the terms of the Trust, you are required to obey all of the laws of the state of Florida relating to the administration of the Trust. For example, Florida law requires that you account to the beneficiaries of the Trust and keep them reasonably informed of how the Trust it is being administered (FS 737.303, 737.3035). You should consult with an attorney experienced in Estate Planning to help you administer the Trust according to the law and without any liability to yourself.

IF YOU ARE A BENEFICIARY OF THE TRUST
If you are a beneficiary of the Trust, you are entitled to receive a copy of the Trust and to be told how the Trust will be administered now that the Grantor or Settlor is deceased. Most Trust documents are written in legalese," so you may want to employ your own attorney to review the Trust, and explain your rights under the Trust.

People and companies who were doing business with the decedent need to be notified of his death. This includes utility companies, credit card companies, banks, brokerage firms and any company that insured the decedent.

NOTIFY CREDIT CARD COMPANIES

You need to notify the decedent's credit card companies of the death. If you can find the contract with the credit card company, check to see whether the decedent had credit card insurance. If the decedent had credit card insurance, then the balance of the account is now paid in full. If you cannot find the contract, contact the company and get a copy of the contract along with a statement of the balance due as of the date of death.

DESTROY DECEDENT'S CREDIT CARDS

You need to destroy all of the decedent's credit cards. If you hold a credit card jointly with the decedent, then it is important to waste no time in closing that account and opening another in your name only.

That's something Barbara knows from hard experience. She and Hank never married but they did live together for several years before he died from liver disease. Hank came from a well to do family so he had enough money to support himself and Barbara during his long illness. Hank put Barbara on all of his credit card accounts so that she could purchase things when he became too ill to go shopping with her. After the funeral, Barbara had a gathering of friends and family at their apartment. Barbara was so preoccupied with her loss that she never noticed that Hank's credit cards were missing until the bills started coming in.

Barbara did not know who ran up the bills on Hank's credit cards during the month following his death. It was obvious that Hank's signature had been forged — but who forged it? One credit card company suspected that it might have been Barbara herself to get out of paying the bill by saying that the card had been stolen

Because the cards were held jointly, Barbara became liable to either pay the charges to the credit card or prove that she did not make the purchases. She was able to clear her credit record but it took several months and she had to employ an attorney to help her do so.

NOTIFY INSURANCE COMPANIES

Examine the decedent's financial records to determine the name and telephone number of all of the companies that insured the decedent or his property. This includes real property insurance, motor vehicle insurance, health insurance and life insurance.

MOTOR VEHICLE INSURANCE
Locate the insurance policy for any type of motor vehicle owed by the decedent (car, truck, boat, airplane) and notify the insurance company of the death. Determine how long insurance coverage continues after the death. Ask the insurance agent to explain what things are covered under the policy. Is the motor vehicle covered for all types of casualty (theft, accident, vandalism, etc.) or is coverage limited in some way?

If you can continue coverage, then determine when the next insurance payment is due. Hopefully, the car will be sold or transferred to a beneficiary before that date, but if not, you need to arrange for sufficient insurance coverage during the Probate procedure.

LIFE INSURANCE COMPANIES

If the decedent had life insurance, you need to locate the policy and notify the company of his death. Call each life insurance company and ask what they require in order to forward the insurance proceeds to the beneficiary. Most companies will ask you to send them the original policy and a certified copy of the death certificate. Send the original policy by certified mail or any of the overnight services that require a signed receipt for the package. Make a copy of the original policy for your records before mailing the original policy to the company.

BANK ACCOUNT LIFE INSURANCE

Many banks, credit unions, savings and loan associations provide life insurance at no cost to the primary owner of the account. While the amounts are generally small ($1,000 to $5,000), it is insurance that is often overlooked when settling the decedent's affairs. If you do not find a record of such policy, contact each financial institution to determine whether such insurance is provided by the company.

 ACCIDENTAL DEATH

If the decedent died as a result of an accident, then check for all possible sources of accident insurance coverage including his homeowner's policy. Some credit card companies provide accident insurance as part of their contract with their card holders. If the decedent died in an automobile accident, check to see whether he was covered by any type of travel insurance, such as rental car insurance. If he belonged to an automobile club, such as AAA, then check whether he had accident insurance as part of his club membership.

IF YOU CANNOT LOCATE THE POLICY

If you know that the decedent was insured, but you cannot locate the insurance policy, you can contact the company and request a copy of the policy. A tougher question is how to locate the policy if you do not know the name of the insurance company. The American Council of Life Insurers offers suggestions that you may find helpful at the Missing Policy Inquiry page of their Web site:

 AMERICAN COUNCIL OF LIFE INSURERS
http://www.acli.com

IF YOU CANNOT LOCATE THE COMPANY

If you cannot locate the insurance company it may be doing business under another name or it may no longer be doing business in the state of Florida. Each state has a branch of government that regulates insurance companies doing business in that state. If you are having difficulty locating the insurance company you can call the Department of Insurance in the state where the policy was purchased and ask for assistance in locating the company. In Florida you can call the Florida Department of Financial Services Consumer Helpline at (800) 342-2762.

EAGLE PUBLISHING COMPANY OF BOCA has the telephone number of the Department of Insurance for each state at the PUBLIC INFORMATION section its Web site.
http://www.eaglepublishing.com

WORK RELATED INSURANCE

If the decedent was employed, check his records for information about work related benefits. He may have survivor benefits from a company or group life insurance plan and/or a retirement plan. Also check with the employer about company benefits. If the decedent belonged to a union, contact them to determine whether there are any union benefits.

The decedent may have belonged to a professional, fraternal or social organization such as the local Chamber of Commerce, a Veteran's organization, the Kiwanis, AARP, the Rotary Club, etc. If he belonged to any such organization check to see whether the organization provided any type of insurance coverage.

 BUSINESS OWNED BY DECEDENT

If the decedent owned his own company or was a partner in a company, he may have purchased "key man" insurance. Key man insurance is a policy designed to protect the company should a valuable employee become disabled or die. Benefits are paid to the company to compensate the company for the loss of someone who is essential to the continuation of the business. Ultimately the policy benefits those who inherit the business.

If the decedent had an ownership interest in an ongoing business (sole proprietor, shareholder or partner), there may be a shareholder's or partnership agreement requiring the company to purchase the decedent's share of the business. The Personal Representative or his attorney needs to investigate to see if there was a key man insurance policy and/or such purchase agreement.

If the decedent was the sole owner of a corporation and the company stock was in his name only, there may need to be a Probate proceeding before the company can be transferred to the new owner.

Florida statute requires each corporation to continuously maintain a Registered Agent within the state. If the decedent was the sole officer and/or Registered Agent of the company, the Corporations Division of the Office of the Secretary of State needs to be notified of the identity of the new officers and Registered Agent as soon as is practicable (FS 607.0505).

Forms to change officers and/or Registered Agent can be obtained by calling (850) 487-9000 or writing to: THE BUREAU OF CORPORATE RECORDS
P.O. Box 6327
Tallahassee, FL   32314

If you were not actively involved in running the business, you might want to call the Corporations Division for information about the company (names, addresses of officers and directors, number of company shares, whether fees are current, etc.). You can get information about the corporation from the Internet.

FLORIDA DIVISION OF CORPORATION
http://www.sunbiz.org

HOMEOWNER'S INSURANCE

If the decedent owned his own home, then check whether there is sufficient insurance coverage on the property. The decedent may have neglected to increase his insurance as the property appreciated in value. If you think the property may be vacant for some period of time, then it is important to have vandalism coverage included in the policy. Once the property is sold, or transferred to the proper beneficiary, you can have the policy discontinued or transferred to the new owner. The decedent's Estate should receive a refund for the unused portion of the premium.

MORTGAGE INSURANCE

If the decedent had a mortgage on any parcel of real estate that he owned, he might have arranged with his lender for an insurance policy that pays off the mortgage balance in the event of his death. Look at the closing statement to see whether there was a charge for mortgage insurance. Also check with the lender to determine if such a policy was purchased.

If there was no mortgage insurance, and the decedent was the sole owner, the beneficiary of the property needs to make arrangements with the lender to continue making payments on the mortgage or to refinance the loan.

NOTIFY THE HOMEOWNER'S ASSOCIATION

If the decedent owned a condominium or a residence regulated by a homeowner's association, then the association will need to be notified of the death. Once the property is transferred to the proper beneficiary, he will need to contact the association to learn of the rules and regulations regarding ownership. The new owner will need to arrange to have notices of dues and assessments forwarded to him.

HEALTH INSURANCE

The Health Insurance carrier probably knows of the death, but it is a good idea to contact them to determine what coverage the decedent had under that insurance plan. If you cannot find the original policy, have the insurance company send you a copy of the policy so that you can determine whether medical treatment given to the decedent before his death was covered by that policy.

 *Special Situation* **DECEDENT ON MEDICARE**

If the decedent was covered by Medicare, you do not need to notify anyone, but you do need to know what things were covered by Medicare so that you can determine what medical bills are (or are not) covered by Medicare. The government publication MEDICARE AND YOU (Publication No. CMS-10050) explains what things are covered under Medicare and the different kinds of plans that are currently available. You can get the publication by writing to:

U.S. Dept. of Health and Human Services
Centers for Medicare and Medicaid Services
7500 Security Boulevard
Baltimore, MD 21244-1850

You can download the publication from the Internet.

 MEDICARE WEB SITE
http://www.medicare.gov

The publication is available on Audiotape, in Braille, in large print and in Spanish. To receive a copy you can call (800) 633-4227. TTY users call (877) 486-2048.

SPOUSE — THE SPOUSE'S HEALTH INSURANCE

If the spouse of the decedent is insured under Medicare, then the death does not affect the surviving spouse's coverage. If the spouse was not covered by Medicare but has her own health insurance that also covered the decedent, then the spouse needs to notify the employer of the death because this may affect the cost of the plan to the employer and/or the spouse. If the spouse was covered under the decedent's policy then he/she needs to arrange for new coverage. There are state and federal laws that ensure continued coverage under the decedent's policy for a period of time depending on whether the decedent's employer falls under federal or state regulation.

If the decedent was employed by a federally regulated company (usually a company with at least twenty employees), then under the Consolidated Omnibus Budget Reconciliation Act ("COBRA") the employer must make the company health plan available to the surviving spouse and any dependent child of the decedent for at least 36 months. The employer is required to give notice to the surviving spouse that the spouse and/or dependent child have the right to continue coverage under the decedent's health plan. The spouse and/or child have 60 days from the date of death or 60 days after the employer sends notice (whichever is later) to tell the employer whether the surviving spouse and child wish to continue with the health insurance plan (29 U.S.C. Sec. 1162, 1163). The only problem with continued coverage may be the cost. Before the death, the employer may have been paying some percentage of the premium. The employer has no such duty after the death unless there was some employment agreement stating otherwise.

Under COBRA, the employer may charge the spouse for the full cost of the plan plus a 2% administrative fee. If you have a question about your coverage under COBRA, you can call the U.S. Department of Labor ("DOL") at (800) 998-7542 and ask for the number of your local DOL office. You can also ask that they send you their publication HEALTH BENEFITS UNDER COBRA; or you can visit their Web site for more information.

U.S. DEPARTMENT OF LABOR
http://www.dol.gov/dol/pwba

HEALTH INSURANCE COVERAGE UNDER FLORIDA LAW

If the decedent's employer is not regulated under COBRA, and employs less than 20 people, then insurance coverage may be regulated under The Florida Health Insurance Coverage Continuation Act. This law is similar to COBRA, but with different time constraints. Coverage need only continue for 18 months and the spouse or dependent child has just 30 days from the date of death or notice from the employer (whichever is later) to let the employer know that they wish to continue with the coverage. Again, cost may be a problem. Under the Florida statute, the spouse can be charged the full cost of the policy plus an additional 15%. The spouse may find it less costly to seek health insurance elsewhere (FS 627.6692).

You can get information about Florida health insurance coverage by calling The Florida Department of Financial Services Consumer Helpline at (800) 342-2762 or by visiting the Department of Financial Services Web site.

THE FLORIDA DEPT. OF FINANCIAL SERVICES
http://www.fldfs.com/

NOTIFY ADVERTISERS

Probably the last in the world to learn of the decedent's death is the direct mail advertiser. Advertisers are nothing if not tenacious. It is not uncommon for advertisements to be mailed to the decedent for more than ten years after the death. It is not because the advertiser is trying to sell something to the decedent, but rather the people who prepare (and sell) mailing lists do not know that the person is dead.

Those who sell mailing lists may not be motivated to update the list because of the cost of doing the necessary research; and perhaps because the price of the mailing list is often based on the number of people on the list. Even those who compose their own list may decide it is less costly to mail to everyone, than take the time (and money) to update the list.

If it gives you pleasure to think of advertisers spending substantial sums for nothing, then that is what you should do (nothing). But for those of you who wince each time you see another piece of mail addressed to the decedent, you can write to the Direct Marketing Association and ask that the name be deleted from all mailing lists:

Mail Preference Service
Direct Marketing Association
P.O. Box 9008
Farmingdale, NY 11735

You will need to give them the decedent's complete address, including zip code and every name variation that the decedent may have used; for example:

Mr. Theodore James Jones
Ted Jones   Ted J. Jones
T. J. Jones   T. James Jones, etc.

✍ CHANGE BENEFICIARIES ✍

If the decedent was someone you named as beneficiary of your insurance policy, Will or trust, brokerage account or pension plan, then you may need to name another beneficiary in his place:

INSURANCE POLICY ✍

If you named the decedent as the primary beneficiary of your life insurance policy, check to see whether you named a contingent (alternate) beneficiary in the event that the decedent did not survive you. If not, you need to contact the insurance company and name a new beneficiary. If you did name a contingent beneficiary, that person is now your primary beneficiary and you need to consider whether you wish to name a new contingent beneficiary at this time.

HEALTH INSURANCE POLICY ✍

If the decedent was covered under your health insurance policy, your employer and the health insurer need to be notified of the death because this may affect the cost of the plan to you and/or your employer.

WILL OR TRUST ✍

Most Wills provide for a contingent beneficiary in the event that the person named as beneficiary dies first. If you named the decedent as your beneficiary, check to see whether you named an alternate beneficiary. If not, you need to have your attorney revise your Will and name a new beneficiary.

Similarly, if you are the Grantor or Settlor of a Trust and the decedent was one of the beneficiaries of your Trust, check the Trust document to see if you named an alternate beneficiary. If not, contact your attorney to prepare an amendment to the Trust, naming a new beneficiary.

BANK AND SECURITIES ACCOUNTS ✍

If the decedent was a beneficiary or joint owner of your bank or securities account, it is important to contact the financial institution and tell them about the death. You may wish to arrange for a new beneficiary or joint owner at this time.

PENSION PLANS ✍

If the decedent was a beneficiary under your pension plan, you need to notify them of his death and name a new beneficiary. Many pension plans require that you notify them within a set period of time (usually 30 days) so it is important to notify them as soon as you are able. If the decedent was a beneficiary of your Individual Retirement Account ("IRA") or of your Qualified Retirement Plan ("QRP") and you did not provide for an alternate beneficiary, you need to name another at this time.

Before you choose an alternate beneficiary, it is important that you understand all of the options available to you. Not an easy task. There are many complex government regulations relating to IRA and QRP accounts. Even if you believe you understood your options when you set up your account, the federal government often changes those options.

Your choice of beneficiary might impact the amount of money you can withdraw each month, so it is important to consult with your accountant or tax attorney or financial planner, before you make your election.

NOTIFYING CREDITORS

It is the job of the person appointed as Personal Representative to notify the decedent's creditors of the death so that the creditor is given an opportunity to come forward and file a *claim* (a written demand for payment) for monies owed. The attorney for the Personal Representative usually takes care of the notice procedure. We will explain that procedure later in this book.

If no Probate proceeding is necessary, the next of kin can notify the creditors of the death, but before doing so, it is important to read Chapter 4: WHAT BILLS NEED TO BE PAID? That chapter explains what bills need to be paid and who is responsible to pay them.

Before any bill can be paid, you need to know whether the decedent left any asset that can be used to pay those debts. The next chapter explains how to identify, and then locate all of the property owned by the decedent.

Locating the Assets 3

It is important to locate the financial records of the decedent and then carefully examine those records. Even the partner of a long-term marriage should conduct a thorough search because the surviving spouse may be unaware of all that was owned (or owed) by the decedent.

It is not unusual for a surviving spouse to be surprised when learning of the decedent's business transactions, especially in those cases where the decedent had control of family finances. One such example is that of Sam and Henrietta. They married just as soon as Sam was discharged from the army after World War II. During their marriage, Sam handled all of the finances giving Henrietta just enough money to run the household.

Every now and again Henrietta would think of getting a job. She longed to have her own source of income and some economic independence. Each time she brought up the subject Sam would loudly object. He had no patience for this new "woman's lib" thing. Sam said he got married to have a real wife — one who would cook his meals and keep house for him.

Henrietta was not the arguing type. She rationalized, saying that Sam had a delicate stomach and dust allergies. He needed her to prepare his special meals and keep an immaculate house for him. Besides, Sam had a good job with a major cruise line and he needed her to accompany him on his frequent business trips.

Once Sam retired, he was even more cautious in his spending habits. Henrietta seldom complained. She assumed the reason for his "thrift" was that they had little money and had to live on his pension.

They were married 52 years when Sam died at the age of 83. Henrietta was 81 at the time of his death. She was one very happy, very angry and very aged widow when she discovered that Sam left her with assets worth well over a million dollars!

LOCATING RECORDS

As you go through the papers of the decedent you may come across documents that indicate property ownership, such as bank registers, stock or bond certificates, insurance policies, pension or annuity records, etc. Place all evidence of ownership in a single place. You will need to contact the different companies in order to transfer title to the proper beneficiary.

To obtain the property, you may need to produce evidence of the decedent's personal relationships, such as a marriage or birth certificate, or naturalization papers, or military personnel records. If you cannot locate the decedent's marriage or birth certificate, you can get a copy of those records from the Vital Records office in the state where the event took place. Many states restrict access to these records to close family members or to the decedent's Personal Representative. See chapter 1 for the telephone number of Florida's Vital Records office. You can find the location and telephone number of the Vital Records of other states by calling information or you can use the Internet to locate the office by using your favorite search engine to find Vital Statistics or Vital Records.

You can obtain a copy of the military record of a deceased veteran by writing to:

The National Personnel Records Center
Military Personnel Records
9700 Page Avenue
St. Louis, MO   63132-5100

They will send you form SF 180 to complete. You can get the form from the Internet at http://www.cem.va.gov or from the National Archives and Records Administration Fax-On-Demand system. Dial (301) 713-6905 and request document number 2255.

COLLECT AND IDENTIFY KEYS

The decedent may have kept his records in a safe deposit box, so you may find that your first job is to locate the keys to the box. As you go through the personal effects of the decedent, collect and identify all the keys that you find. If you come across an unidentified key, it could be a key to a post office box (private or federal) or a safe deposit box located in a bank or in a private vault company. You will need to determine whether that key opens a box that contains property belonging to the decedent or whether the key is to a box no longer in use. Some ways to investigate are as follows:

☑ CHECK BUSINESS RECORDS

If the decedent kept receipts, look through those items to see if he paid for the rental of a post office or safe deposit box. Also, look at his check register to see if he wrote a check to the Postmaster or to any safe deposit or vault company. Look at his bank statements to see if there is any bank charge for a safe deposit box. Some banks bill separately for safe deposit boxes so check with all of the banks in which the decedent had an account to determine if he had a safe deposit box with that bank.

☑ CHECK THE KEY TYPE

If you cannot identify the key, then take it to each local locksmith and ask whether anyone can identify the type of facility that uses such keys. If that doesn't work, go to each bank, post office and private safe deposit box company where the decedent shopped, worked or frequented and ask whether they use the type of key that you found.

☑ CHECK THE MAIL

Check the mail over the next several months to see if the decedent receives a statement requesting payment for the next year's rental of a post office or safe deposit box.

You may find evidence of a brokerage account, bank account, or safe deposit box by examining correspondence addressed to the decedent. If the decedent was living alone, have his mail forwarded to the person he named as Personal Representative or Executor of his Will. If the decedent did not leave a Will, and no Probate procedure is necessary, the mail should be forwarded to his next of kin. Call the Postmaster and ask him to send you the necessary forms to make the change. Request that the mail be forwarded for the longest period allowed by law (currently one year).

The decedent may have been renting a post office box at his local post office branch or perhaps at the branch closest to where he did his banking. Ask the Postmaster to help you determine whether the decedent was renting a post office box. If so, then you need to locate the key to the box so that you can collect the decedent's mail.

Special Situation **LOST POST OFFICE BOX KEY**

If the decedent had a post office box and you cannot locate the key, contact the local postmaster and ask him what documentation is needed for you to gain possession of the mail in that box. As before, you will ask the Postmaster to have all future mail addressed to that box, forwarded to the Personal Representative, or if no Probate is necessary, to the decedent's next of kin.

WHAT TO DO WITH CHECKS

You may receive checks in the mail made out to the decedent. Social Security checks, pension checks and annuity checks issued after the date of death may need to be returned to the sender. (See pages 32 and 34 of this book.) Other checks need to be deposited. If a Probate procedure is necessary, then the Personal Representative will open a Probate Estate account and will deposit the decedent's checks to that account.

If no Probate procedure is necessary, then checks can be deposited to any account held in the name of the decedent. The decedent is not here to endorse the check, but you can deposit it to his account by writing his bank account number on the back of the check and printing beneath it **FOR DEPOSIT ONLY.**

The bank will accept such an endorsement and deposit the check into the decedent's account. If the check is significant in value or the decedent had different accounts that are accessible to different people, then there needs to be cooperation and a sense of fair play. If not, the dollar gain may not nearly offset the emotional turmoil.

Such was the case with Gail. Her father made her a joint owner of his checking account to assist in paying his bills. He had macular degeneration and it was increasingly difficult for him to see. The father also had a savings account that was in his name only.

Gail's brother Ken had a good paying job in Alaska. Even though he lived at a distance, Ken, his wife and two children always spent the Christmas holidays with his father and sister.

Each summer, their father enjoyed leaving the heat of Florida to spend a few weeks in the cool Alaskan climate.

One summer, the father purchased a round trip ticket to Alaska. It cost several hundred dollars. Just before the departure date, the father had a heart attack and died. Gail called the airline to cancel the ticket. They refunded the money in a check made out to her father. She deposited the check to the joint account, and then closed it out.

As part of the Probate procedure, the money in the father's savings account was divided equally between Ken and his sister. Ken wondered what happened to the money from the airline tickets.

Gail explained "Dad paid for the tickets from the joint account, so I deposited the money back to that account. "

"Aren't you going to give me half?"

"Dad meant for me to have whatever was in that joint account. If he wanted you to have half of the money, he would have made you joint owner as well."

Ken didn't see it that way "That refund was part of Dad's Estate. It should have been deposited to his savings account to be divided equally between us. Are you going to force me to argue this in Court?"

Gail finally agreed to split the money with Ken, but the damage was done.

Gail complains that holidays are lonely since Dad died.

LOCATE FINANCIAL RECORDS

To locate the decedent's assets you need to find evidence of what he owned and where those assets are located. His financial records should lead you to the location of all of his assets, so your first job is to locate those records. The best place to start the search is in the decedent's home. Many people keep their financial records in a single place but it is important to check the entire house to be sure you did not miss something.

CHECK THE COMPUTER

Don't overlook that computer sitting silently in the corner. It may hold the decedent's check register and all of the decedent's financial records. Check his e-mail for e-bank or on-line credit accounts. The computer may be programmed to protect information. If you cannot access the decedent's records, you may need to employ a computer technician or consultant who will be able to print out all of the information on the hard drive of the computer. You can find such a technician or consultant by looking in the telephone book under COMPUTER SUPPORT SERVICES or COMPUTER SYSTEM DESIGNS & CONSULTANTS.

 **LAWYER**   DECEDENT'S
ONGOING BUSINESS

If the decedent was the sole owner of a business, or if he owned a partnership interest in a business, the Personal Representative needs to contact the company accountant to obtain the company's business records. If there is a company attorney, then the attorney may be able to assist in obtaining the records. If you are a beneficiary of the Estate, consider consulting with your own attorney to determine what rights and responsibilities you may have in the business.

LOCATE TITLE TO MOTOR VEHICLE

In Florida, if monies are owed on a motor vehicle (car, mobile home or trailer), the lender takes possession of the original certificate of title until the loan is paid. If you cannot find the original certificate of title, it is either lost or monies are owed on the car and the lienholder has the original title. You can go to the Motor Vehicle Office in the county of the decedent's residence and they will issue a replacement (duplicate) title to you. The Motor Vehicle Office will require proof of your authority to get a copy of the Title. In some cases, they will issue the replacement title only to the Personal Representative. It is a good idea to first call the Department of Highway Safety and Motor Vehicles (850) 922-9000 for information about what documents they require and the cost of obtaining the replacement Title. If you find there is a loan on the car, contact the lienholder and get a copy of the contract that is the basis of the loan.

THE LEASED CAR
You may find that the car is leased and not owned by the decedent. If so, contact the lessor and get a copy of the lease agreement. Check to see whether the decedent had life insurance as part of the agreement. If he did, the lease may now be paid in full and the beneficiary of the car should be able to use the car for the remainder of the leasing period, or take title to the car, whichever option is available under the lease agreement. The Personal Representative (or the beneficiary) can send the death certificate to the leasing company with a copy of the contract and a letter requesting that the transfer be made. If the lease is not paid in full upon the decedent's death, then arrangements need to be made to satisfy the terms of the agreement. See Chapter 6 for information about transferring a leased car.

Mobile homes that are driven on the road are titled and registered in the same manner as any other motor vehicle (FS 320.02). See the previous page if you cannot locate the certificate of title to the mobile home. Homes that are permanently attached to a parcel of land do not need to be registered. See Chapter 6 for information about transferring the land and the mobile home to the proper beneficiary. If the decedent owned a mobile home that is kept in a leased space, you need to locate the lease to the mobile home lot. If you cannot locate the lease, contact the landlord for a copy, and proceed in the same manner as for a residential lease.

 Special Situation   **DECEDENT'S RESIDENTIAL LEASE**

If the decedent was renting his residence, he may have a written lease agreement. It is important to locate the lease because the decedent's Estate may be responsible to continue payment under the lease. Ask the landlord for a copy if you cannot locate the lease. If the landlord reports that there was no written lease, then verify that the decedent was on a month to month basis and work out a mutually agreeable time in which to vacate the premises.

If a written lease is in effect, determine the end of the lease period, and whether there was a security deposit. Ask whether the landlord will agree to cancel the lease on the condition that the property is left in good condition. If the landlord wants the Estate to be responsible to pay the balance of the lease, then it is prudent to have an attorney review the lease to determine what rights and responsibilities remain now that the tenant is deceased.

LOCATE TITLE TO MOTOR BOATS

All motor boats 16 feet in length, or greater, that are used primarily in the state of Florida must be registered with the Florida Department of Highway Safety and Motor Vehicles, with the exception of vessels that are registered with the federal government such as the U.S. Coast Guard (FS 328.03). If the decedent owned a boat that he used principally in Florida, and you cannot locate his registration, you can apply for a duplicate registration at your local motor vehicle office. You will need to show proof of ownership by showing them the boat's certificate of title. If the title certificate is also missing, you will need to obtain a duplicated certificate from the County Tax Collector (FS 328.01).

LOCATE TITLE TO AIRCRAFT

If the decedent owned an aircraft, then you should find a certificate of title to the aircraft. The Civil Aviation Registry of the Federal Aviation Administration ("FAA") contains all of the ownership and security documents that have been filed with the FAA. If you cannot locate title to the aircraft you can contact the Civil Aviation Registry. They do not perform title searches, however they can give you a list of title search companies. If you wish to perform the title search yourself you can call the Aircraft Registration Branch at (405) 954-3116 for more information or you can visit the FAA Web site.

 THE FEDERAL AVIATION ADMINISTRATION
http://www2.faa.gov

COLLECT DEEDS

Collect deeds to all of the property owned by the decedent. In addition to the deed, look for other documents associated with the property, such as a mortgage. You may come across a Title Insurance policy. The new owner might be able to turn in that policy and receive a discount toward the purchase of a new title insurance, so it is important to keep the policy together with the deed.

Instead of a title insurance policy you may find an **Abstract of Title**. An Abstract of Title is a summary of the documents or facts appearing on the public record which affect title to the property. The Abstract will need to be updated once the property is transferred. We will discuss the transfer of property in Chapter 6.

Many people keep deeds in a safe deposit box. If you cannot find the deed in the decedent's home, then you need to determine whether he had a safe deposit box and if so, you need to examine the contents of the box. See the end of this chapter for information about how to access the decedent's safe deposit box.

If you know that the decedent owned real property (lot, residential property, condominium) but you cannot find the deed, contact the recording department in the county where the property is located. The Clerk of the Circuit Court is in charge of recording. The Clerk can provide you with a copy of the last recorded deed. You might want to call the Clerk to determine how to obtain a copy of the deed. You can find the telephone number of the Clerk of the Circuit Court at the state of Florida Web site.

 STATE OF FLORIDA
http://www.myflorida.com

LOCATING THE
OUT OF STATE DEED

You need to locate the deed and any related document (Abstract of Title, title insurance policy, recorded condominium approval, etc.) to out of state property owned by the decedent.

THE LOST OUT OF STATE DEED

If you know the decedent owned out of state real property, but cannot find the deed, you can use the same procedure just described, namely, you can check with the recording department in the county where the property is located. In Florida, the Clerk of the Circuit Court is in charge of the recording department. In other states it may be the County Recorder or Registrar of Deeds. The Clerk in the recording department should be able to give you a copy of the last recorded deed.

Many states index the property by the name of the current owner of the property, so if you know the county where the property is located, you should be able to find the deed by giving the decedent's name to the Clerk.

If you do not know the county in which the property is located, you will need to wait for the next tax bill. In many states the tax bill contains its legal description, or tax identification number.

The decedent's final federal income tax return needs to be filed so you should look for his tax records for the past three years. If you cannot locate his prior tax records, check his personal telephone book and bank register to see if he employed someone to prepare his taxes. If you can locate his tax preparer, then he should have a copy of those records.

If you are unable to locate the decedent's incomel tax returns, they can be obtained from the IRS. The IRS will send copies of the decedent's tax filings to anyone who has a *fiduciary relationship* with the decedent. The IRS considers the following people to be a fiduciary:

➤ the person appointed as the Personal Representative of the decedent's Estate

➤ the Successor Trustee of the decedent's Trust

➤ if the person died without a Will, whoever is legally entitled to possession of the decedent's property. See Chapter 5 for an explanation of the Laws of Intestate Succession.

The fiduciary can receive copies of the decedent's tax filings by notifying IRS that he is acting in a fiduciary capacity, and then requesting the copies.

To notify the IRS of the fiduciary capacity file Form 56:
NOTICE CONCERNING FIDUCIARY RELATIONSHIP

Your accountant can file these forms for you or you can obtain the forms from the IRS by calling (800) 829-3676 or you can download them from the FORMS section of the IRS Web site.

 INTERNAL REVENUE SERVICE
http://www.irs.gov

FLORIDA INTANGIBLE TAX RETURN

The state of Florida has an annual Intangible Tax on securities owned by residents of the state (FS 199.032). If you are having difficulty locating the decedent's assets and you suspect he had a significant amount of securities (stocks, bonds, etc.), look at his last Intangible Tax Return to find out what securities he owned at the time of the filing. If you cannot find his last tax return, the Personal Representative (or next of kin, if he died without a Will) can write to the Florida Department of Revenue and request a copy of the decedent's last Intangible Tax Return.

FLORIDA DEPARTMENT OF REVENUE
PERMANENT RECORDS SECTION
5050 West Tennessee Street
Tallahassee, FL 32399-0100

Before writing, you may want to call the Intangible Tax Department at (850) 488-9925 and ask what information or document they may require for you to obtain a copy of the return.

LOCATE OUT OF STATE ACCOUNTS

If the decedent had out of state bank or brokerage accounts, then you might be able to locate them if they mail out monthly or quarterly statements. Not all financial institutions do so, but all institutions are required to send out an IRS tax form 1099 each year giving the amount of interest earned on that account. Once the forms come in, you will learn the location of all of the decedent's active accounts.

If the decedent was forgetful, he may have money in a lost bank account or abandoned safe deposit box. Property that is unclaimed is turned over to the Florida Department of Financial Services after a period of time as set by Florida law. The time period depends on the item:.

- ⧗ 1 year for unclaimed wages

- ⧗ 1 year after service is discontinued for an unclaimed utility deposit

- ⧗ 3 years after the lease has expired for the contents of a safe deposit box

- ⧗ 5 years after monies are payable under a life insurance policy or annuity

- ⧗ 5 years for a cashier's check, Certificate of Deposit, or last transaction on a bank account

- ⧗ 15 years from the date of issue of a travelers check (FS 717.105, 717.106, 717.107, 717.108, 717.115 717.116, 717.122).

Before turning the property over to the state, the holder of the unclaimed property must make a good faith effort to contact the owner and return the property to him. Once the Department of Financial Services has possession of the item, they will try to locate the owner as well. If a tangible item (such as jewelry) remains unclaimed, the Department will convert it to cash by holding a public auction either on the Internet, or at a specified location, whichever the Department thinks is the most favorable market for the property. If the owner, or his heirs, later claim the item, they will receive the proceeds of the sale, less the cost of selling the item (FS 717.12405).

You can determine whether there is a record identifying the decedent as the owner of abandoned property by calling (888) 258-2253 or writing to:

THE FLORIDA DEPARTMENT OF FINANCIAL SERVICES
ABANDONED PROPERTY SECTION
200 E. Gainses Street
Tallahassee, FL 32399-0350

You can also get information from Consumer section of the Department of Financial Services Web site.

 FLORIDA DEPARTMENT OF FINANCIAL SERVICES
http://www.fldfs.com

CLAIMS IN OTHER STATES

Each state has an agency or department that is responsible for handling lost, abandoned or unclaimed property located within that state. If the decedent had residences in other states, then call the UNCLAIMED or ABANDONED PROPERTY department of the state Comptroller or Treasurer to see if the decedent has unclaimed property in that state. EAGLE PUBLISHING COMPANY OF BOCA lists telephone numbers for the unclaimed property division for each state at the Public Information section of their Web site.

http://www.eaglepublishing.com

CLAIMS FOR DECEDENT VICTIMS OF HOLOCAUST

The New York State Banking Department has a special Claims Processing Office for Holocaust survivors or their heirs. The office processes claims for Swiss bank accounts that were dormant since the end of World War II. If the decedent was a victim of the Holocaust, you can get information about money that may be due to the decedent's Estate by calling (800) 695-3318.

CLAIMS FOR INCOME TAX REFUNDS

The IRS reports that some 90,000 tax refund checks representing 67.4 million dollars were returned to them as being not deliverable. They keep the information on file and will forward the full amount once they locate the taxpayer. You can determine whether they are holding a check for the decedent by calling the IRS at (800) 829-1040 or by visiting their Web site.

 U.S. TREASURY
http://irs.ustreas.gov

THE LOST PENSION

The decedent may be entitled to benefits under a pension plan of a prior employer. If the decedent worked for an employer for any significant period of time, say five years or more, then you need to check with the company benefit representative to determine whether any pension funds are payable. If you are unable to locate the former employer, it could be that the company moved or merged with another company. There are several ways to track down the company, starting with the Secretary of State to learn of the company's current status (see page 50).

CONTACT THE UNION
If company workers belonged to a union, you can contact the union.They may be able to help you locate the company, or tell you what happened to the pension funds.

CONTACT SOCIAL SECURITY

The Social Security Administration has the decedent's work record and the employer identification number for each of his employers. The Personal Representative should be able to get that information by calling the Social Security Administration at (800) 772-1213.

Using the employer identification number you might be able to determine whether the pension fund has been taken over by another company.

RESEARCH THE INTERNET

Pension Benefit Guaranty Corporation insures private sector pensions. They operate an on-line search tool for those employees whose pension plans were closed because of bankruptcy, or because the company dissolved the plan, or because the company could not locate the employee. You can search their Web site by employee name or by the company name.

 PENSION BENEFIT GUARANTY CORPORATION
http://www.pbgc.gov/search

LOCATE CONTRACTS

If the decedent belonged to a health club or gym, he may have prepaid for the year. Look for the club contract. It will give the terms of the agreement. If you cannot locate the contract, contact the company for a copy of the agreement. If the contract was prepaid, determine whether the agreement provides for a refund for the unused portion.

Even if the contract does not provide for a refund, you may be able to get the owner of the gym to agree to assigning the remaining membership to an heir of the decedent's Estate. Such an assignment is good public relations as well as a means of generating new business should the heir decide to purchase his own membership.

SERVICE CONTRACT

Many people purchase appliance service contracts to have their appliances serviced in the event that an appliance should need repair. If the decedent had a security system , he may have had a service contract with a company to monitor the system and contact the police in the event of a break-in.

If the decedent had a service contract, you need to locate it and determine whether it can be assigned to the new owner of the property. If the contract is assignable, the new owner can reimburse the decedent's Estate for the unused portion. If the contract cannot be assigned, then once the property is transferred, try to obtain a refund for the unused portion of the contract.

FILING THE WILL

Anyone who has possession of the decedent's original Will should deposit it with the Probate Court in the county of the decedent's residence. If the decedent owned property in Florida, but did not live here, then the Will needs to be deposited with the Probate Court in the county where the decedent's property is located. Anyone who has the original Will and who fails to or refuses to deposit the Will with the Probate Court, after being notified of the death, can be sued for any loss suffered because of that failure or refusal (FL 732.901, 733.101).

The judge of the Probate Court will accept an original Will only and not a copy, so it is important to hand carry the original document to the Court. If you are the Personal Representative of the Will, you can give it to your attorney to file with the court as part of the Probate procedure. Make a copy of the Will for your own records before delivering it to the Court or to your attorney.

Special Situation | WILL DRAFTED IN ANOTHER STATE OR COUNTRY

The state of Florida respects the laws of other states and countries. If a Will is drafted in another state or country and the Will is valid in that state or country, it is valid here, provided the Will is in writing and there is at least one person who signed as a witness to the Will (FS 732.502). If the Will is written in a foreign language, it must be accompanied by a true and complete English translation before it can be admitted to Probate (FS 733.204).

 **LAWYER**

PROBATING THE OUT OF STATE PROPERTY

If the decedent had his residence in Florida and owned property in another state, you may need to conduct the initial Probate in Florida and an *ancillary* (secondary) Probate in the other state. If the decedent had his residence in another state and owned property in Florida, then it may need to be the other way around; namely, you may need to conduct the initial Probate in the other state and an ancillary proceeding here (FS 734.102).

If you are going to be Personal Representative, and the decedent owned property in another state or was a resident of another state, then before depositing the Will with the Court you should consult with an experienced Probate attorney in each state to deter mine where the initial Probate should be conducted. Convenience is important, but there are other things you need to consider

COST OF PROBATE Ask each attorney whether the location of the initial Probate procedure will have an effect on the total cost of Probate.

WHO INHERITS THE INTESTATE ESTATE Intestate laws vary significantly state to state. If the decedent died without a Will, it is important to determine whether the location of the initial Probate procedure will change the amount each heir will inherit.

ESTATE/INHERITANCE TAXES You need to determine whether the location of the initial procedure will have an impact on the amount of taxes that need to be paid.

THE MISSING WILL

People tend to put off making a Will until they think they need to. For many, that need arises when they are elderly and/or seriously ill and have property that they want to leave to someone. It is uncommon for a young person to have a Will; but those who are aged, and with significant assets, usually have one. A survey conducted for the American Association of Retired Persons ("AARP") found that the probability of having a Will increases with age. Forty-four percent of those surveyed who were between the ages of 50 to 54 had a Will. This increased to 85% for those 80 and older. You can find details of the survey at the AARP Web site.

AARP WEB SITE
http://research.aarp.org

Those who make a Will usually tell the person they appoint as Executor of the existence of the Will. Chances are, that someone in the decedent's circle of family and friends, knows whether there is a Will. If you believe that the decedent had a Will, but you cannot find it, there are at least three places to check out:

⇨   **THE DECEDENT'S ATTORNEY**
Look at the decedent's checkbook for the past few years and see whether he paid any attorney fees. If you are able to locate the decedent's attorney, then call and ask whether he ever drafted a Will for the decedent, and if so, whether he has the original Will in his possession. If he does, ask him to forward it to the Probate Court in the county of the decedent's residence. Asking the attorney to forward the Will to the court does not obligate you employ the attorney should you find that you need the assistance of an attorney for the Probate administration.

⇨ THE CLERK OF THE PROBATE COURT

Florida law requires that whoever has the original Will must deposit it with the Probate Court within 10 days after learning of the death. The Court understands that it may take more than 10 days after the date of death to locate the document, but once it is located, whoever has it in his possession, must deposit it with the Clerk of the Circuit Court of the Probate Division. Anyone who fails to deposit the Will, without good reason for the delay, can be held liable to the decedent's Estate for the legal costs of forcing them to deposit the Will with the Court (FL 732.901).

It is a good idea to check with the Clerk in the county where the decedent lived in the chance that someone found the Will and filed it with the Court.

⇨ THE SAFE DEPOSIT BOX

Most people keep their original Will in a safe deposit box. If you believe that the decedent had a Will but you cannot find it, then check to see if the decedent had a safe deposit box. If he did, you will need to gain entry to that box to see whether the Will is in the box. See page 84 for an explanation of how to gain entry to the safe deposit box.

 **LAWYER**

A COPY OF THE WILL
AND NO ORIGINAL

A person can revoke his Will simply by destroying it i.e., by ripping it up, or by writing over it in such a manner as to indicate that the Will is cancelled or revoked (FS 732.506). If you have a copy of the Will and cannot find the original, the Probate Judge will presume that the decedent revoked his Will by destroying it. If you believe the original was not revoked but is lost, you can ask the Probate Court to admit a copy of the Will to Probate.

Florida courts have allowed a lost Will to be probated provided it can be proven that:

☑ the document offered is a true copy of the original Will, AND

☑ the decedent did not intend to revoke the Will (FL 733.207).

Not easy things to prove. If you wish to have a lost Will admitted to Probate, you will need to employ an attorney experienced in Probate matters to present your case to the Court.

ACCESSING THE SAFE DEPOSIT BOX

If the decedent rented a safe deposit box with another person, each with free access to the box, then the surviving joint renter of the box can go to the box and remove the contents of the box. If the decedent had a safe deposit box and he was the only person with access to the safe deposit box, under Florida law, the bank (or safe deposit box lessor) may allow any of the following people to examine the contents of the box:

> ▶ the decedent's spouse

> ▶ a parent of the decedent

> ▶ an adult descendant

> ▶ the person named as Personal Representative in a copy of the decedent's Will
> (FS 655.935)

Florida statute requires that an officer, manager or assistant manager of the bank be present when the safe deposit box is opened.

If you are any of the above persons and you need to get into the safe deposit box, then call the bank ahead of time and make an appointment to meet with an officer of the company.

If you are gaining access because you are named as the Personal Representative or Executor of the Will, then you need to bring a copy of the Will with you. Ask the bank what other identification they will require of you. Most companies require that you bring a certified copy of the death certificate, so you may need to wait until you receive the death certificate to prove to the bank officials that the owner of the box is dead.

If the original Will is found in the box, then upon your request the bank will deliver the Will to the Probate Court in the county of the decedent's residence. If the decedent's primary residence was not in Florida, the Will can be probated in the county in Florida where the safe deposit box is located.

If there is a deed to the decedent's burial plot in the safe deposit box, the officer of the bank can give that deed to you. Also, if there is a life insurance policy in the safe deposit box, the bank has the authority to give the policy to the beneficiary named in the policy. Nothing else may be removed from the safe deposit box until the Personal Representative is appointed and takes possession of the decedent's Probate Estate (FS 655.935).

If you find other valuables in the box that need to be removed from the box, you may need to go through some kind of Probate procedure to get possession of those items. See Chapter 6 for an explanation of what type of Probate procedure may be necessary in order to get possession of the contents of the decedent's safe deposit box.

Once you have located the decedent's property you may think the next step is to determine who gets to inherit that property. But some of that property may be needed to pay monies owed by the decedent; so the next step is to determine what, if any, bills need to be paid. And that is the topic of the next chapter.

What Bills Need To Be Paid? 4

The Personal Representative has the duty to be sure that all valid claims against the Estate (demands for payment) are paid. If the decedent had debts, but no money or property, then of course, there is no way to pay the claim. The only remaining question is whether anyone else is responsible to pay for the monies owed. If the decedent was married, the first person the creditor will look to is the decedent's spouse. To understand the basis of this expectation, you need to know a bit of the history of our legal system.

Our laws are derived from the English Common Law. Under early English Common Law, a single woman had the right to own property in her own name and also the right to contract to buy or sell property; but when she married, her legal identity merged with her spouse. She could not hold property free from her husband's claim or control. She could no longer enter into a contract without her husband's permission.

Once married, a woman became financially dependent on her husband. He, in turn, became legally responsible to provide his wife with basic necessities — food, clothing, shelter and medical services. If anyone provided basic necessities to his wife, then, regardless of whether the husband agreed to be responsible for the debt, he became obliged to pay for them. This law was called the DOCTRINE OF NECESSARIES.

States in America departed from English Common Law by enacting a series of Married Women's Rights Acts. The state of Florida passed the Married Women's Rights law giving a married woman the right to own property and to enter into a contract without her husband's permission (FS 708.08).

After the Married Women's Rights law was passed, a series of cases tested whether the Doctrine of Necessaries still applied in the state of Florida. Court cases followed that tested whether the Doctrine of Necessaries still applied. Judges had to decide:

If a wife can own property and contract to pay for her own necessities, should her husband be responsible for such debts in the event she does not have enough money to pay for them?

And if it is determined that the husband is responsible for his wife's necessities, should she be responsible for his?

In Florida the answer was "no" to both questions (*Connor vs. Southwest Florida Regional Medical Center, Inc.*, 668 So.2d 175 (Fla. 1995)). The Court reasoned that because a wife has the right to own property and to enter into her own contracts, the husband should not be responsible to pay for his wife's necessities unless he agrees to do so. The Court also ruled that because of the principal of equality under the law, in Florida, the wife is not liable for her husband's debts unless she agrees to pay for them Under current Florida law neither partner is responsible to pay for the necessities of the other. If the spouse who made the contract or purchase, does not have sufficient funds to pay, then his/her spouse is not responsible for the debt unless the spouse agrees to do so.

JOINT DEBTS

A *joint debt* is a debt that two or more people are responsible to pay. Usually the contract or promissory note states that the parties agree to *joint and several liability*, meaning they all agree to pay the debt and each of them promises to be personally responsible to pay the debt. A joint debt can also be in the form of monies owed by one person with payment guaranteed by another person. If the person who owes the money does not pay, then the *guarantor* (the person who guaranteed payment) is responsible to make payment. Nursing home bills, funeral expenses, legal fees to Probate the decedent's Estate are all debts of his Estate. They are not joint debts unless someone guaranteed payment for monies owed.

PAYING FOR THE JOINT DEBT

If another person is jointly responsible for monies owed by the decedent, that bill should be paid from any joint account held with the decedent. If the joint debtor did not have a joint account with the decedent, the joint debtor must pay the bill from his/her own funds.

SPOUSE ➤ JOINT SPOUSAL DEBTS

Loans signed by the decedent and his spouse are joint debts, as are charges on credit cards that both were authorized to use. Property taxes are a joint debt if the decedent and the spouse both owned the property.

Suppose all of the decedent's funds are held jointly with his spouse or a family member and the joint owner of the account did not agree to pay those debts? Can the creditor require that half of the joint funds be set aside to pay the debt?

The answer to this question depends on how the joint property is titled. As we will see in Chapter 5 there are different ways to hold property jointly with another. If the property is held *jointly with rights of survivorship*, the surviving owner owns the property as of the date of death. If there is no right of survivorship, the creditor has the right to demand that the decedent's share be used to pay the debt.

Under Florida statute 655.79, unless the bank account states otherwise, it is presumed that a deposit account (including CD's) in two or more names, is a joint account with rights of survivorship. If a Florida bank account is a joint account, then as of the date of death the money in that account belongs to the surviving owner or owners of the account.

BUT NOT EXEMPT FROM UNCLE SAM

The surviving owner(s) have no obligation to use the joint account funds to pay the decedent's creditors because the funds are not part of the decedent's **Probate** Estate. However, the decedent's share of the joint account is included as part of the decedent's **Taxable** Estate, so if Estate Taxes are due to the federal and state government, the remaining owners of the joint account will need to contribute their share of the tax bill (FS 733.817).

If the decedent owed money then the debt needs to be paid from assets owned by the decedent — which leads to the next question "Did the decedent have any money in his own name when he died?"

If the decedent died without any money or property in his name, then there is no money to pay any creditor. The only question that remains is whether anyone else is liable to pay those bills. The issue of payment most often arises in relation to services provided by nursing homes. When a person enters a nursing home, he is usually too ill to speak for himself or even sign his name. In such cases, the nursing home administrator will ask the spouse or a family member to sign a battery of papers on behalf of the patient before allowing the patient to enter the facility. Buried in that battery of papers may be a statement that the family member agrees to be responsible for payment to the nursing home. If the family member refuses to guarantee payment and the patient's finances are limited, then the facility may refuse to admit the patient.

Under the Federal Nursing Home Reform Law, a nursing home that accepts Medicare or Medicaid payments is prohibited from requiring a family member to guarantee payment as a condition of allowing the patient to enter that facility (42 U.S.C. 1395I-3(c)(5)(A)(ii)). None the less, it is common practice for a nursing home, in effect, to say "Either someone agrees to pay for the patient's bill or you need to find a different facility."

Their position is understandable, in light of the fact that even if the patient is married, the nursing home cannot require payment from the spouse unless the spouse agrees to be responsible for monies owed. Most nursing homes are business establishments and not charitable organizations. The nursing home must be paid for the services they provide or they soon will be out of business. For an insolvent patient, the solution to the problem is to have the patient admitted to a facility as a Medicaid patient.

But suppose the decedent had some money when he entered the nursing home and you agreed to guarantee payment to the nursing home. What if you feel that you were coerced into signing as a guarantor?

Are you now liable to pay the decedent's final nursing home bill if your family member died without funds?

An experienced Elder Law attorney will be able to answer these questions after examining the documents that you signed and the conditions under which the patient entered the nursing home.

PAYING THE DECEDENT'S BILLS

If the decedent was married and no Probate procedure is necessary, then the surviving spouse needs to make provision for paying bills they were both responsible to pay. If the decedent was not married and he owned property belonging to him alone, such as a bank account, securities or real property, then paying monies owed by the decedent falls to the Personal Representative.

Just as soon as he is appointed, the Representative is required to make a diligent effort to locate all of the decedent's creditors and notify them that they need to file their written claim with the Clerk of the Probate Court. Any creditor who is not given written notice can file their claim anytime within two years from the date of death (FS 733.212).

The Personal Representative needs to look over each claim and decide whether that claim is valid. The problem with making that decision is that the decedent is not here to say whether he actually received the goods and services that are now being billed to his Estate. That is especially the case for medical or nursing care bills. An example of improper billing brought to the attention of this author was that of a bill submitted for a physical examination of the decedent. The bill listed the date of the examination as July 10th, but the decedent died on July 9th. Other incorrect billings may not be as obvious, so each invoice needs to be carefully examined. If the Personal Representative decides to challenge a bill he must notify the creditor in writing that he objects to the bill. The creditor then has 30 days to file a law suit in Civil Division (FS 733.705). If the law suit is successful, the Personal Representative must pay the amount ordered by the Court.

MEDICAL BILLS COVERED BY INSURANCE

If the decedent had health insurance you may receive an invoice stamped "THIS IS NOT A BILL." This means the health care provider has submitted the bill to the decedent's health insurance company and expects to be paid by them. If the decedent was receiving Medicare, you will receive a *Medicare Summary Notice* listing all of the services or supplies that were billed to Medicare for the prior 30 days. In some areas of the country, you can get a copy of the decedent's Medicare Summary Notice from the Internet. To see if it is available in your area, look up e-MSN in the "Frequently Asked Questions" section of the Medicare Web site http://www.medicare.gov.

Even though payment is not requested, it is important to verify that the bill is valid for two reasons:

➤ LATER LIABILITY

If the insurer refuses to pay the claim, the facility will seek payment from whoever is in possession of the decedent's property, and that may reduce the amount inherited by the beneficiaries.

➤ INCREASED HEALTH CARE COSTS

Regardless of whether the decedent was covered by a private health care insurer or Medicare, improper billing increases the cost of health insurance to all of us. Consumers pay high premiums for health coverage. We, as taxpayers, all share the cost of Medicare. If unnecessary or fraudulent billing is not checked, then ultimately, we all pay.

If you believe you have come across a case of Medicare fraud, you can call the ANTI-FRAUD HOTLINE (800) 447-8477 and report the incident to the Office of the Inspector General of the United States Department of Health and Human Services.

HOW TO CHECK MEDICARE BILLING

The structure of Medicare has been changed giving people in some parts of the country, the option of staying with the *Original Medicare Plan* or choosing one of the *Medicare Advantage Plans*. Health care coverage depends on which plan is chosen. If the decedent was covered by Medicare, you need to determine whether he was covered under the Original Medicare Plan, or whether he chose a Medicare Advantage Plan. The publication *Medicare and You* explains coverage under the different options. See page 51 to obtain a copy of the booklet.

Coverage under a Medicare Advantage Plan is explained in the membership materials given to the decedent at the time he signed up for the plan.

BILLING UNDER THE ORIGINAL MEDICARE PLAN

ASSIGNMENT

An important billing question for those under the Original Medicare Plan is whether the health care provider agreed to accept Medicare *assignment*, meaning that they agreed to accept the Medicare-approved amount. If so, the patient is responsible for the coinsurance rate (usually 20% of the approved amount) and any deductible amount. Doctors and health care providers who do not accept assignment, are limited in the amount they can charge for a Medicare covered service. The highest they can charge is **15%** over the Medicare-approved amount. This *Limiting Charge* applies only to certain services and does not apply to supplies and equipment. For more information about assignment you can call (800) 633-4227 for your free copy of *Does your doctor or supplier accept "assignment?"* or you can down-load the publication from the Medicare Web site.

http://www.medicare.gov

ADVANCE BENEFICIARY NOTICE

For those who are in the Original Medicare Plan, a doctor or a supplier may give notice saying that Medicare probably will not pay for the service that is about to be provided. This is called an *Advance Beneficiary Notice*. If the patient still wants the service after receiving such Notice, he will be asked to sign an agreement stating that he will pay for the service, in the event that Medicare does not pay.

If all of this appears confusing, it is.

To check the decedent's Medicare billing, you need the answers to the following questions:

What is the plan?

Determine whether the decedent was in the Original Medicare Plan or in one of the Medicare Advantage Plans.

What is covered under the plan?

The *Medicare and You* booklet explains what is covered under the Original Medicare Plan. You will need a copy of the membership materials for the Medicare Advantage Plans to determine what is covered under that plan.

Does the Provider accept Assignment?

If the decedent was in the Original Medicare Plan, you need to determine whether the health care provider accepted assignment; and if not whether the Limiting Charge applies to the services provided. If assignment is accepted or the Limiting Charge applies, you need to determine the Medicare-approved amount.

Did the decedent agree to pay?

If the decedent was in the Original Medicare Plan, check to see whether the decedent was given an Advance Beneficiary Notice; and if so, whether he signed a contract agreeing to pay in the event that Medicare refuses to pay.

| Special Situation | DENIAL OF MEDICARE COVERAGE |

If the health care provider reports to you that a service provided to the decedent is not covered by Medicare, or if the facility submits the bill and Medicare refuses to pay, check to see if you agree with that ruling by finding answers to the questions on the prior page. You can appeal that decision if you believe that the decedent was wrongly denied coverage.

If the decedent was in the Original Medicare Plan, you will find information about how to file an appeal on the Medicare Summary Notice. If he was part of the Medicare Advantage, you will find that information in his health care plan materials.

GETTING HELP WITH THE APPEAL

You can appeal the decision yourself, but it is best to seek assistance. The **Florida Department Of Elder Affairs** has created an agency called **SERVING HEALTH INSURANCE NEEDS OF ELDERS ("SHINE")** to assist people with their Medicare appeals. This service is free of charge. Call the Elder Help-Line at **(800) 963-5337** for the telephone number of the **SHINE** office nearest you.

If you want an attorney to assist with your appeal, call the Florida Bar at (800) 342-8011 for a referral to an attorney experienced in Medicare appeals. Some attorneys work *pro bono* (literally for the public good; i.e. without charge) but most charge to assist in an appeal. Federal statute 42 U.S.C. 406(a)(2)(A) limits the amount an attorney may charge for a successful Medicare appeal to 25% of the amount recovered or $4,000, whichever is the smaller amount.

Medicaid is a program that provides medical and long term nursing care for people with low income and limited resources. The program is funded jointly by the federal and state government. Federal law requires the state to recover monies spent from the Estate of a Medicaid recipient who was 55 or older when the decedent received Medicaid assistance. The state will seek reimbursement for the cost of nursing home care or for home based care or for other community based services (42 U.S.C. 1396(p)).

There usually is no money to recover because to qualify for Medicaid in Florida, a person may not have more than $2,000 in assets. But sometimes it happens that person on Medicaid dies and his Estate later receives money perhaps as part of a settlement of a lawsuit. Also, it could happen that he owned a home. Owning a home does not disqualify a person from receiving Medicaid, however if he received Medicaid benefits after age 55, the state has the right to place a lien on that home and seek recovery from the proceeds of the sale of the house once he dies. Federal law prohibits any recovery of monies, until the surviving spouse, and/or disabled child of the decedent are deceased.

The Personal Representative needs to notify **THE AGENCY FOR HEALTH CARE ADMINISTRATION** that the state has a right to file a claim against the Estate to recover monies spent for the benefit of the decedent (FS 733.2121). He can call the decedent's caseworker or the Department of Children and Family Services for information about where to send the notice.

SOME THINGS ARE CREDITOR PROOF

Sometimes it happens that the decedent had money or property titled in his name only, but he also had a significant amount of debt. In such cases the beneficiaries may wonder whether they should go through a Probate procedure if there will be little, if anything, left after the creditors are paid. Before making the decision consider that some assets are protected under Florida law:

✧ PENSION PLANS ✧

Annuities, pensions, profit sharing or other retirement plans regulated by the federal Employee Retirement Income Security Act of 1974 ("ERISA"), including IRA accounts and plans identified by the Internal Revenue Code as 401(a) and 403(a & b), 408, 408A and 409 are creditor proof. Monies received by a beneficiary of such plans are protected from the decedent's AND beneficiaries creditors with the following exceptions:

NO EXEMPTION FOR TAXES

In general, income taxes are not paid when money is placed in a retirement plan. Taxes are paid when the monies are withdrawn from the account regardless of whether the monies are withdrawn by the retiree or the person he named as beneficiary of the retirement plan. If your beneficiary inherits money from your pension, retirement allowance, or annuity, he may need to pay taxes on those monies.

NO EXEMPTION FOR QUALIFIED DOMESTIC RELATIONS ORDER

If a Court has ordered the decedent or beneficiary to pay funds to his family under a Qualified Domestic Relations Order, then the pension funds are available to make such payment (FS 222.21).

✧ BENEFITS TO TEACHER OR ADMINISTRATOR ✧

The state of Florida provides a death benefit of $75,000 to any teacher or school administrator who is killed in his line of duty as the result of an intentional act of violence. If the teacher has not named a specific beneficiary for the death benefit, then the money is paid to the decedent's Estate. In addition, $1,000 will be paid toward the decedent's funeral or burial expenses These funds are exempt from the claims of the decedent's creditors (FS 112.1915).

✧ FINAL WAGES ✧

The decedent's employer can pay wages and travel expenses that are due, directly to the surviving spouse. If there is no spouse, the employer can pay the funds to the decedent's adult children; and if no children, then to his parents. All of the wages and up to $300 in travel expenses go to these family members free from the claims of the creditors of the decedent. If none of these family members survive the decedent, the funds become part of his Probate Estate and available to pay any valid claim (FS 222.15, 222.16).

✧ LIFE INSURANCE PROCEEDS ✧

Life insurance proceeds paid to a beneficiary as a result of the decedent's death are exempt from the claims of the decedent's creditors; however if the proceeds of the policy are payable to the decedent or to his Estate, then those proceeds become part of his Probate Estate and are available to pay his debts (FS 222.13, 222.14).

✧ EXEMPTIONS FOR SURVIVING SPOUSE ✧

The decedent's surviving spouse and/or minor children are entitled to take certain items of the decedent's Estate free from the claims of any of his creditors.

THE HOMESTEAD EXEMPTION ✧

Florida property owned and occupied by a person as his/her main residence is called *homestead* property. Article X Section 4 (a) of the Florida Constitution protects the homestead from forced sale by creditors. Should the owner of the homestead die, creditor protection of his home continues for his spouse or family members who inherit the homestead.

There are exceptions to this rule. Creditor protection does not extend to delinquent taxes or mortgages on the homestead or to mechanics' liens. But in general, if all that the decedent owned was his homestead, the decedent's creditors will not be able to force the sale of the homestead to pay those debts.

This exemption is unlimited, meaning that if the homestead is worth a million dollars, then one million dollars of the decedent's Estate is creditor proof. There is a bill being considered in the United States Congress, which if passed, would limit a Homestead Exemption, to $100,000, but as of this writing, in Florida, the Homestead Exemption is unlimited.

EXEMPT PERSONAL PROPERTY ✧

The surviving spouse is entitled to take the following *Exempt Property* free from the decedent's creditor claims, except for monies owed on any given item:

⇨   all automobiles held in the decedent's name and regularly used by the decedent or his family as their personal automobile

⇨   household furniture, furnishings, and appliances up to $10,000 in value

⇨   any Florida Prepaid College Program contract.

If there is no surviving spouse, the decedent's children inherit these items free from creditor claims. If the decedent made a gift of any Exempt item in his Will, it is no longer Exempt Property. However, if the gift was made to the surviving spouse, or if no spouse, to his children, the beneficiary can ask the Court to allow it to keep its Exempt status (FS 732.402).

THE FAMILY ALLOWANCE ✧

The decedent's spouse is to receive a *Family Allowance* for his/her maintenance during the Probate proceeding. The decedent's dependent descendants (children, grandchildren, etc.) are also entitled to an Allowance for their maintenance during Probate. Up to $18,000 of the Probate Estate can be paid as a Family Allowance. It can be paid as a single lump sum or it can paid monthly. The Court determines the value of the Family Allowance and to whom it should be paid (FS 732.403).

As explained on the next page, the Family Allowance is free from creditor claims, with the exception of the cost of administering the Probate proceeding, funeral and burial expenses, taxes, and the reasonable medical expenses of the last 60 days of the decedent's illness.

Next, consider that not all Probate debts are equal. If there are insufficient funds in the Probate Estate to pay for all claims against the decedent's Estate, then Florida Statute (FS 733.707) establishes an order of priority for payment:

CLASS 1:   COST OF ADMINISTRATION

Top priority goes to the cost of the probate proceeding including attorney's fees and fees charged by the Personal Representative.

CLASS 2:   FUNERAL EXPENSES

Second in priority is the decedent's funeral, burial and grave marker expenses but only up to $6,000. Anything over $6,000 becomes a Class 8 debt.

CLASS 3:   FEDERAL/STATE

Taxes owed to the federal government by the decedent are Class 3 debt. The state has a right to be reimbursed for medical assistance provided to the decedent after age 55. The state claim is a Class 3 obligation, however, this claim can be waived by the state in the event that its collection would cause undue hardship for the beneficiaries of the Estate such as being deprived of basic necessities of food, clothing, shelter or medical care (FS 409.9101).

CLASS 4:   MEDICAL

Reasonable and necessary medical and hospital expenses of the last 60 days of the decedent's last illness are 4th in line for payment.

CLASS 5: FAMILY ALLOWANCE

If the decedent was a Florida resident and he was supporting a spouse or *lineal heirs* (children, grand-children, parents or grandparents of decedent), then the dependents can receive up to $6,000 for their maintenance during the Probate of the Estate.

CLASS 6:   CHILD SUPPORT

If the decedent was, by court order, responsible for child support and was late with those payments, then the monies owed are 6th in priority.

CLASS 7:   BUSINESS CONTINUATION DEBTS

Debts associated with continuation of the decedent's business after his death for up to four months — but only to the extent of the value of the business assets.

CLASS 8:   ALL OTHER DEBTS

Any excess over the sums allowed for Class 2 and Class 4 debts are a Class 8 debt. All other claims, including judgments against the decedent during his lifetime are eighth in line for payment.

Florida law 733.707 requires that claims against the Probate Estate be paid in the above order. For example, suppose the decedent left enough money to pay for the Probate, his funeral, and his taxes (the first 3 classes) with $10,000 left over. If there are no other debts then the beneficiaries get the $10,000.

Suppose instead that he had no other debts except $15,000 in credit card debts and $4,000 in back child support. In that case, the child's surviving parent can ask the Probate Court for the Family Allowance ($6,000) and for the remaining $4,000 as partial payment of monies owed for child support. If the court so orders, no money will be left over to pay the credit card debt (a Class 8 debt). No money will be left for any other beneficiary.

✧ THERE IS A STATUTE OF LIMITATIONS ✧

There are federal and state laws that set time periods for pursuing a claim. Anyone who wishes to take court action must do so within the time set by the given Statute of Limitation. For example, a law suit for the wrongful death of the decedent must be filed within two years of the death (FS 95.11).

There is a Statute of Limitations for a creditor to come forward and make a claim against the decedent's Estate for monies owed. The Personal Representative must publish a Notice To Creditors in the newspaper for two consecutive weeks to inform any unknown creditor of the death. Creditors then have 3 month to file their claim with the Court. He will also mail notice to any of the decedent's known creditors (FS 733.2121, 733.702).

But what if no one starts a Probate procedure?

Florida Statute 733.710 states that if a claim is not filed within two years after the death, that claim cannot be enforced against the Estate, the Personal Representative, or any of the beneficiaries.

There are exceptions to the two-year limit such as mortgages and federal claims and certain liens on the decedent's property. But, in general, if no one begins a probate proceeding until two years have passed, the beneficiaries may be able to obtain possession of the decedent's assets free from creditor claims.

Some may be thinking that it may be a good idea to postpone Probate until two years have passed.

Read on before you decide to wait for two years.

 **☎ LAWYER**

DECEDENT LEAVING CONSIDERABLE DEBT

If the decedent died leaving much debt and no property, the solution is simple. No Probate, no one gets paid. But if the decedent had property and died owing more money than the property was worth, his heirs may decide that going through Probate is not worth the effort, or they may decide to simply wait out the two year Statute of Limitation period and begin Probate at that time.

This may not be the best decision. Some creditors are tenacious and will use whatever legal strategy is available in order to be paid, including initiating the Probate proceeding themselves. If no one starts the Probate, a creditor can ask the Court to be appointed Personal Representative of the Estate (FS 733.202).

As we will see in Chapter 6, a Personal Representative has much authority when conducting the Probate procedure. Family members may object to having a creditor as a Personal Representative, so there could be a court battle over who has priority to be appointed as Personal Representative. Court battles are expensive, emotionally as well as financially. Before you decide to distance yourself from the Probate proceeding, consult with an attorney experienced in Probate matters for an opinion about the best way to administer the Estate.

MONIES OWED TO THE DECEDENT

Suppose you owed money to the decedent. Do you need to pay that debt now that he is dead? That depends on whether there is some written document that says the debt is forgiven once the decedent dies. For example, suppose the decedent loaned you money to buy your home. If he left a Will saying that once he dies, your debt is forgiven, then you do not need to make any more payments. If you signed a promissory note and mortgage at the time you borrowed the money from the decedent, the Personal Representative should sign the original promissory note **PAID IN FULL** and return the note to you. If the mortgage was recorded, the Personal Representative needs to have a Satisfaction of Mortgage recorded in the county where the property is located. You should receive the recorded Satisfaction for your records.

If you owed the decedent money and there is no Will, or if there is a Will, and no mention of forgiving the debt, then you still owe the money. Monies borrowed from the decedent and his spouse need to be repaid to the spouse. Monies borrowed from the decedent only, become an asset to the estate of the decedent, meaning that you owe the money to the decedent's Estate. If you are one of the beneficiaries of the Estate, you can deduct the money from your inheritance.

For example, suppose your father left $70,000 in a bank account to be divided equally among you and your two brothers. If you owed your father $20,000, your father's Estate is really worth $90,000. Instead of paying the $20,000, you can agree to receive $10,000 and have the $20,000 debt forgiven. Each of your brothers will then receive $30,000 in cash.

Who Are The Beneficiaries? 5

A question that comes up early on is who is entitled to the property of the decedent. To answer the question you first need to know how the property was titled (owned) as of the date of death.

There are three ways to own property. The decedent could have owned property jointly with another person; or in trust for another person; or the decedent could have owned property that was titled in his name only.

In general, upon the decedent's death:

Joint Property with Right of Survivor
belongs to the surviving joint owner.

Trust Property belongs to the beneficiary
of the Trust.

Property owned by the **decedent only** is inherited
by the beneficiaries named in the Will.
If there is no Will, then the property goes to his heirs
according to Florida's Laws of Intestate Succession.

NOTE ⇨ If the decedent was married, his
spouse may have rights in his property.

This chapter describes each type of ownership in detail.

PROPERTY OWNED JOINTLY

Bank accounts, securities, motor vehicles, real property can all be owned jointly by two or more people. If one of the joint owners dies, the survivor(s) continue to their share of the property. Who owns the share belonging to the decedent depends on how the joint ownership was set up.

THE JOINT BANK ACCOUNT

When a bank account is opened the depositors sign an agreement with the bank that states the term and conditions of the account. Under Florida statute (FL 655.79) a bank account or a certificate of deposit that is titled in two or more names, is presumed to be a survivorship account. If the decedent and another person are joint owners of an account — each with the ability to withdraw funds on his own signature, the surviving owner of that account is free to withdraw all of the funds and close it out. If both signatures are necessary to make a withdrawal, the joint owner will need to present a certified copy of the death certificate to the bank to obtain possession of the funds in the account.

Although the surviving owner is free to take possession of the account, he needs to be aware that he may be responsible to pay Estate Taxes on money that he inherits from the account (see Chapter 2). If a joint account is held in three names, each with authority to make withdrawals, the share owned by the decedent is divided equally between the surviving owners. Of course, either of the survivors can go to the bank and withdraw all of the funds in the account. With such an arrangement, the surviving owners need to cooperate with each other to divide the funds in the account equitably.

You can determine whether the decedent owns a security alone or jointly with another by examining the face of the stock or bond certificate. If two names are printed on the certificate followed by a statement that the owners are "Joint Tenants With Rights of Survivorship ("JTWRS")," then the surviving owner can either cash in the security or ask the company to issue a new certificate in the name of the surviving owner.

Each state has its own securities regulations. If a security held in two or more names, was registered or purchased in another state, and it does not indicate whether there are rights of survivor, you need to contact the company to determine how the account was set up; i.e. with or without rights of survivorship.

If the decedent held his securities in a brokerage account, then the name of the owner of that account is printed on the monthly or quarterly brokerage statement. Not all brokerage firms print the name of a joint owner on the brokerage statement, so you need to contact the firm to determine whether there is a surviving joint owner, or perhaps a beneficiary of the account. Request a copy of the contract that is the basis of the account. The contract will show when the account was opened and the terms of the brokerage account.

JOINTLY OWNED MOTOR VEHICLE

If a motor vehicle is owned jointly, the name of each owner is printed on the title to the motor vehicle. Joint ownership is indicated by the words "AND" or "OR," for example, the title can read: HENRY LEE OR SUSAN LEE
or title can read: HENRY LEE AND SUSAN LEE.

In either case, if one person dies, the other owns the car. If Henry dies, all Susan need do is bring the title certificate and a certified copy of Henry's death certificate to her local Department of Highway Safety and Motor Vehicles and they will issue a new title certificate identifying Susan as the owner of the car.

We will discuss the transfer of motor vehicles in the next chapter, but see the Office Locator section of the Department Web site for a complete listing of the locations of their locations.

 DEPT. OF HIGHWAY SAFETY & MOTOR VEHICLES
http://www.hsmv.state.fl.us

REAL PROPERTY OWNED JOINTLY

The name of the owner of real property is printed on the face of the deed. To determine whether the decedent owned the property jointly with another person, you need to look at the last recorded deed. The deed will indicate joint ownership. For example:

This indenture, made this day, March 15, 2004,
between ROSEANNE TRAYNOR, a single woman,
party of the first part
hereinafter referred to as the Grantor, and
ALFRED CODY, SR. and ALFRED CODY, JR.,
as JOINT TENANTS WITH RIGHTS OF SURVIVORSHIP
parties of the second part,
hereinafter referred to as the Grantee ....."

Roseanne Traynor is the *Grantor* of the deed. That means she transferred the property to Alfred Cody and Scott Cody who are the *Grantees* and present owners of the property. The deed states that Alfred and Scott are JOINT TENANTS WITH RIGHTS OF SURVIVORSHIP. Should one of the Grantees die, the surviving joint tenant will own the property 100%. Nothing need be done to establish this ownership, however the decedent's name remains on the deed.

If you are the surviving joint owner of real property you may want to have a death certificate recorded to notify anyone who examines title to the property that there is now just one owner. See Chapter 6 for information about transferring title to real property.

▤ DEED HELD AS TENANT IN COMMON

If a deed identifies the decedent and another as TENANTS IN COMMON, then the decedent's share of the property belongs to whomever the decedent named as his beneficiary in his Will. If the decedent died without a Will, the beneficiary of the decedent's property is determined by Florida's Laws of Intestate Succession. With or without a Will, a Probate proceeding will be necessary to transfer the share to the proper beneficiary.

THE AMBIGUOUS DEED
Most deeds clearly state whether the joint owners of the property intend a surviving owner to inherit the decedent's share. For example:

DAN ROGOW and PETER ROGOW,
as Tenants In Common

means that there are no rights of survivorship.

But: DAN ROGOW and PETER ROGOW

or

DAN ROGOW and PETER ROGOW as Joint Tenants

or

DAN ROGOW and PETER ROGOW, jointly

are not all that clear.

According to Florida statute, no right of survivorship exists unless the document clearly states so. That being the case, each of the above examples have no right of survivorship and are the same as a Tenancy In Common (FS 689.15).

There may be other documents available showing that the parties intended this to be a Joint Tenancy With Rights of Survivorship, so if you have any question about who has the right to inherit the property, it is best to consult with an attorney.

🖹 DEED HELD AS HUSBAND AND WIFE

If the Grantee on the deed is identified as a married couple, for example: TODD AMES AND SUSAN AMES, HIS WIFE
or

TODD AMES AND SUSAN AMES, H/W

or

TODD AMES AND SUSAN AMES, HUSBAND AND WIFE

or

TODD AMES AND SUSAN AMES, TENANTS BY ENTIRETY

then this is the same as a joint tenancy with rights of survivorship. When one spouse dies, and providing they are married at the time of death, the surviving spouse owns the property 100% even though the deed still shows the two names. (FS 732.401(2)). The surviving spouse should have the death certificate recorded and that will establish that there is just one owner.

 **LAWYER**

DIVORCED PRIOR TO DEATH

In Florida, if a couple divorce, real property that they owned as Tenants By The Entirety becomes property owned by the couple as Tenants In Common (FL 689.15). Generally, the Final Judgment states who is to own the property after the divorce. If one of the parties died before the deed to their property was transferred to the proper owner, you need to consult with an attorney to determine who now owns the property.

 **LAWYER**   THE OUT OF STATE DEED

The laws of the state or country where the property is located determine who inherits property in that state. If the decedent owned property in another state or country, then even if the decedent was a resident of Florida, the laws of the state where the property is located determine who inherits property in that state.

The laws of each state are similar, but not the same. Laws differ in how the deed needs to be worded in order to have a Right of Survivorship. Some states, such as Georgia, do not require the deed to specifically say there is a Right Of Survivorship. In such states a deed held as Joint Tenant means that there are Rights of Survivorship, even if the deed does not say so. Other states, like Florida, require the deed to say whether there is a Right of Survivorship, and if not, it is a Tenancy In Common.

The rights of married couples varies significantly state to state. If the decedent was married, and owned property in his name only in another state, his surviving spouse may have rights in that property. That may be the case in Community property states. In other states, a surviving spouse may have Dower rights or other statutory rights in the property.

If the decedent owned property in another state, it is important to consult with an attorney in that state to determine who now owns the property.

▤ DEED WITH A LIFE ESTATE

A *Life Estate* interest in real property means that the person who owns the Life Estate has the right to live in that property until he/she dies. You can identify a Life Estate interest by examining the face of the deed. If somewhere on the face of the deed you see the phrase RESERVING A LIFE ESTATE to the deceased Grantor, then the Grantee now owns the property. For example, suppose the granting paragraph of the deed reads:

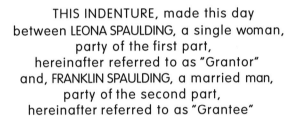

THIS INDENTURE, made this day
between LEONA SPAULDING, a single woman,
party of the first part,
hereinafter referred to as "Grantor"
and, FRANKLIN SPAULDING, a married man,
party of the second part,
hereinafter referred to as "Grantee"

. . .

RESERVING A LIFE ESTATE TO THE GRANTOR

Leona is the owner of the Life Estate. Franklin owns the *Remainder Interest* in the property. Franklin has no right to occupy the property during Leona's lifetime, but once she dies, he will own the property 100%. He will be free to take possession of the property or transfer it, as he sees fit. As with a Joint Tenancy with Right of Survivorship, nothing need be done to establish Franklin's ownership of the property, however he might want to record a copy of Leona's death certificate to show that he now has the right to occupy, sell or transfer the property.

| SPOUSE | AN INVISIBLE LIFE ESTATE |

If the decedent was married and the deed to his homestead was in the decedent's name only, then according to Florida statute 732.401, the spouse has the right to live in that home until he/she dies. This means that regardless of what the deed says, the spouse has a Life Estate interest in that homestead.

Florida statute 732.702 allows the spouse to *waive* (give up) the Life Estate interest. If there is a properly executed pre-nuptial or post-nuptial agreement that waives the Life Estate interest, then the surviving spouse does not have any right to the homestead. See Page 129 for a discussion about the inheritance of the Florida homestead.

 THERE COULD BE A LATER DEED

The above discussion on the different types of ownership of real property assumes that you are in possession the most recent, valid deed. The decedent could have signed another, later deed. Before you come to a conclusion about who inherits the property it is advisable to have a title search by an attorney or a title insurance company to determine the owner of the property as of the decedent's date of death.

BANK/ SECURITY ACCOUNTS

A bank account or security account that is registered in the name of the decedent "In Trust For" or "for the benefit of" someone will be turned over to the beneficiary once the financial institution has a certified copy of the death certificate. If the beneficiary is a minor, and the account balance is under $10,000 the company may give the money to whoever is caring for the child; but if it is over that amount, the company will not transfer the funds without permission from the Probate Court (FS 710.108). Some companies will seek Court approval even if the sum is less than $10,000. See Chapter 7 for a discussion about transfers to minors.

BANK ACCOUNT HELD BY A TRUSTEE

If the bank or security account is registered in the name of the decedent "as Trustee under a Trust Agreement," that means the decedent was the Trustee of a Trust and the bank will turn over that account to the Successor Trustee of the Trust. Banks usually require a copy of the Trust Agreement or a *Certificate of Trust* that identifies the Successor Trustee, so the bank should know the identity of the Successor Trustee. If the Trust was amended to name a different Successor Trustee, you need to present the bank with a copy of that amendment together with a certified copy of the death certificate.

MOTOR VEHICLE

If the motor vehicle is held in the name of the decedent "as Trustee," then the motor vehicle continues to be Trust property. The Successor Trustee will need to contact the motor vehicle bureau to have title changed to that of the Successor Trustee. The Successor Trustee will then dispose of the car according to the terms of the Trust Agreement.

REAL PROPERTY

If the decedent had a Trust and put real property that he owned into the Trust, then the deed may read something like this:

THIS INDENTURE
made this day between
JOHN ZAMORA and MARIA ZAMORA,
his wife, party of the first part,
hereinafter referred to as "Grantor"
and JOHN ZAMORA, **Trustee of the**
JOHN ZAMORA REVOCABLE TRUST AGREEMENT
DATED FEBRUARY 2, 2005,
party of the second part
the following described real property

. . .

The death of the Trustee of a Trust does not change the ownership of the property. It remains in the Trust. The Trust document might say whether the person who takes John's place as Trustee (the Successor Trustee) should sell or keep the property or perhaps give it to a beneficiary. If no instruction is given, the Successor Trustee can use his discretion as to what to do with the property. If you are a beneficiary of the Trust and are concerned about what the Successor Trustee will do with the property, then it is best to consult with your attorney to learn about your rights under that Trust.

If the decedent owned property that was in his name only (not jointly or in trust for someone), then some sort of Probate procedure will be necessary before the heirs can get possession of that property. Who is entitled to the decedent's Probate Estate depends on whether the decedent died with or without a Will. If the decedent died *testate* (with a valid Will), the beneficiaries of the decedent's property are identified in the Will.

If the decedent died without a Will, then Florida's Laws of Intestate Succession determine who inherits the decedent's Probate Estate and what percentage of the Probate Estate each heir is to receive once all the bills and costs of administering the Probate procedure are paid.

The law recognizes the right of the family to inherit the decedent's property. The law covers all possible relationships beginning with the decedent's spouse. The law recognizes the right of the family to inherit the decedent's property. The law covers all possible relationships beginning with the decedent's spouse. But before we discuss the rights of the surviving spouse we need to consider whether decedent had a marriage that is considered as being valid within the state of Florida.

BEING MARRIED IN FLORIDA

To be married in Florida means that a man and a woman have obtained a license to marry from the state, solemnized the marriage by a state or religious ceremony, and then cohabited together as man and wife. Parental consent to marry is required for anyone under 18 but over 16. No one under 16 may marry without Court permission. The Court may issue a license to marry with or without parental consent provided the girl is pregnant or has a child (FS 741.04, 741.0405).

Florida law specifically prohibits the marriage of people who are:

☒   currently married.

Anyone who knows he is married and then deliberately commits bigamy can be convicted of a felony of the third degree (FS 826.01).

☒   related to each other as follows:
⇨   *ancestors* (parent, grandparents, etc.) or *descendants* (child, grandchild, etc.) of each other;
⇨   aunt and nephew or uncle and niece;
⇨   brother and sister (FS 741.21)

Florida law does not bar marriages between cousins.

☒   of the same sex.

Vermont was the first state to recognize a same sex marriage, which they refer to as a "civil union." Several other states, including Florida, have passed statutes, specifically denying marital status to couples of the same gender, regardless of whether that marriage is valid in any other state or country (FS 741.212).

THE COMMON LAW MARRIAGE

A common law marriage is one that has not been solemnized by ceremony. It is more than just living together. The couple must agree to live together as man and wife, and then publicly hold themselves out as being married; i.e., tell friends and family that they are married. Many states no longer recognize a common law marriage as being valid, and have passed laws to that effect. The state of Florida does not recognize a common law marriage that was entered into in the state of Florida after January 1, 1968 (FS 741.211).

Florida respects the laws of other states, so even though common law marriages are no longer valid in Florida, Courts have ruled that they will recognize a common law marriage if it is valid in the state where the couple entered into the marriage *(In Re Estate of Goldfarb*, 502 So.2d 963 (Fla.App. 3 Dist. 1987)).

Now that we know who the state of Florida considers as the surviving spouse, we can determine the rights of the spouse under Florida's Laws of Intestate Succession.

If the decedent died *intestate* (without a Will), the state of Florida provides one for him in the form of its **Laws of Intestate Succession**. Once his debts, funeral expenses, and the cost of the Probate is paid, whatever is left (his *net Probate Estate*) is distributed as follows:

✧ CHILD, NO SPOUSE

If the decedent was single and left descendants (child, grandchild, great-grandchild, etc.), his Net Probate Estate is inherited by his descendants (FS 732.103). If he had two or more children, all who survive him, then each child is entitled to an equal share of his Estate. If a child of the decedent died before the decedent, the share intended for that child goes to the descendants of the deceased child in equal shares. For example, suppose the decedent was unmarried when he died, with four children, Ann, Barry, Carl, David. If he died without a Will, each child get 25% of his Net Probate Estate.

CHILD WITHOUT DESCENDANTS DIES BEFORE DECEDENT

If Ann dies before her father, leaving no descendants, Barry, Carl and David each receive an equal share; i.e., each is entitled to one-third of the Net Probate Estate.

CHILD WITH DESCENDANTS DIES BEFORE DECEDENT

Suppose instead that only Carl and David survived their father. If Ann died leaving no children and Barry died leaving 2 children, then the Estate is divided into 3 shares — one for each surviving child (Carl and David) and one share for Barry's children, who split their share equally.

This method of distributing the decedent's property when a member of a group dies before the decedent is called a *"per stirpes"* distribution.

❖ MARRIED, NO DESCENDANT

If at the time of death the decedent was married and had no surviving *lineal descendants* (children, grandchildren, great-grandchildren, etc.), all of his Estate goes to his surviving spouse.

❖ MARRIED, WITH DESCENDANT

If the decedent was survived by lineal descendants, all of whom are the children of the surviving spouse, then the spouse gets the first $60,000 of the Probate Estate, plus half of the balance of the net Probate Estate. The other half goes to the lineal descendants, in equal shares, per stirpes. If the decedent had surviving lineal descendants, some of whom are not those of his spouse, then the spouse does not get the first $60,000, instead the spouse takes half of the Probate Estate and the decedent's lineal descendants take the other half in equal shares, per stirpes (FS 732.102).

❖ SINGLE, NO DESCENDANTS

If the decedent had no children, the property is divided equally between his parents. If only one of his parents is alive, all of the property goes to that parent. If neither parent is alive, then Estate goes to the decedent's brothers and sisters in equal shares, per stirpes. If the decedent had whole blood siblings and half blood siblings, the half blood sibling inherits only half as much as whole blood sibling (FS 732.108).

For example if the decedent's property is inherited by his brother of the same parents and two sisters of the same father but different mothers, the brother gets half of the Estate and each sister gets one quarter of the Estate.

If the decedent had no brothers, sisters, nephews or nieces, the Probate Estate is divided with half going to his maternal grandparents (or to the survivor of them) and the other half to his paternal grandparents (or the survivor of them). If neither maternal grandparent survived the decedent, then their half goes to their descendants in equal shares, per stirpes; i.e., to the aunts and uncles or to the descendants of a deceased aunt or uncle (i.e., his cousins).

The other half goes to the next of kin on the decedent's father's side in the same manner. If there are next of kin on one side of the family only, the entire Probate Estate is inherited by the next of kin on that side of the family (FS 732.103).

NO RELATIVES BUT A DECEASED SPOUSE
If a person dies without a Will and he has absolutely no surviving relation, but he has a deceased spouse, his Estate goes to the next of kin of his last deceased spouse.

FLORIDA: HEIR OF LAST RESORT
Property that is either unclaimed or abandoned, goes to the state, so if the decedent died without a Will and absolutely no one who could inherit the property under the Laws of Intestate Succession, then the state of Florida "inherits" the net Probate Estate. It will be paid to the Treasurer of the state, who will deposit it into the State School Fund (FS 732.107).

CAUTION IT ISN'T ALL THAT SIMPLE

The explanation in this book of the Laws of Intestate Succession is abridged. Even though you may now know more about Florida's Laws of Intestate Succession than you care to know, there is much more to the law. For example, we did not give specific examples of how the Estate is distributed if the decedent is survived only by descendants of his grandparents. We could give an example explaining the law, but we thought you might enjoy a puzzle instead:

Winston died intestate leaving $100,000 in securities. His only relatives are his mother's sister, Aunt Susie, and her children, Ramona and Abigail and a first cousin Elvis, on his father's side. How much does each relative receive?

You can check your answer by visiting the puzzle section of the Eagle Publishing Company Web site:
http://www.eaglepublishing.com

Those who try the given puzzle will appreciate how complex the Florida Laws of Intestate Succession can be. Unless the descent is straight forward, with the decedent leaving a surviving spouse and/or children (all who survive him), it is best to consult with an attorney before you decide who is entitled to inherit the decedent's intestate property.

Under Florida law anyone who is found guilty of the murder of the decedent, or who is found guilty of being an accessory to the crime is prohibited from profiting from the crime. Property that the killer, or accessory would have inherited as a beneficiary of the decedent's Will, or according to the Florida Laws of Intestate Succession, will be distributed as if the killer died before the decedent (FS 732.802)

There are no rights of survivorship for the killer. Upon the Court determination of guilt, property that was owned by the decedent and the killer, as Joint Property with Right of Survivor, becomes a Tenancy In Common, insofar as the killer and the decedent are concerned. Any other person who is a joint owner of the property, remains a joint owner.

Similarly if the killer is a beneficiary of the decedents life insurance policy or annuity, whoever is named as alternate beneficiary will get the insurance proceeds. If no alternate beneficiary is named, then the proceeds go to the Estate of the decedent.

WHO INHERITS THE HOMESTEAD?

Florida has special (some say quirky) laws relating to the inheritance of the homestead. Article X, Section 4 (c) of the Florida Constitution reads as follows:

> The homestead shall not be subject to devise if the owner is survived by spouse or minor child, except the homestead may be devised to the owner's spouse if there be no minor child.

What ???

Maybe Florida statute 732.401 (1) can shed some light on the subject:

> If not devised as permitted by law and the Florida Constitution, the homestead shall descend in the same manner as other intestate property; but if the decedent is survived by a spouse and lineal descendants, the surviving spouse shall take a Life Estate in the homestead, with a vested remainder to the lineal descendants in being at the time of the decedent's death.

And maybe not.

Even lawyers struggle with the meaning of the Florida homestead laws. So much so, that there have been numerous court cases and many learned treatises on the subject of who has the right to inherit homestead property. The following page contains a summary of current legal opinion as to the meaning and effect of the Florida homestead statute as it relates to the decedent.

SINGLE, NO MINOR CHILD

If the decedent was single, with no minor child at the time of his death, then he had the right to *devise* (leave in his Will) his homestead to whomever he wished. This means that if he left his homestead to a beneficiary, that person inherits the property. If the decedent died without a valid Will, his heirs will inherit the homestead according to Florida's Laws of Intestate Succession.

SINGLE, WITH MINOR CHILD

If the decedent was single and had one more minor children, regardless of what he puts in his Will, that homestead goes to the decedent's children, in equal shares. If the decedent dies without a valid Will, the children still inherit the homestead, in equal shares.

MARRIED

If the decedent was married and their Florida residence owned as husband and wife, the property is owned by the surviving spouse. If the decedent was married and the homestead was in the decedent's name only, then unless the surviving spouse signed a pre-nuptial or post-nuptial agreement giving up homestead rights, he/she has the right to live in the home for the rest of his/her life. Once the spouse dies, the home goes to the decedent's children who were alive at the time of his death, in equal shares. If there were no children alive at the time of his death, the surviving spouse inherits and owns the homestead at the time of the decedent's death.

The above discussion is intended only as an introduction to the subject. If you have any question about who inherits the homestead, then it is important to consult with an experienced Probate attorney.

THE RIGHTS OF A CHILD

THE NON-MARITAL CHILD

A child born out of wedlock has the same rights to inherit from his/her natural father as does one born in wedlock, provided any one of the following are true:

☑   He and the mother participated in a marriage ceremony before or after the birth, even though the marriage is not valid for some reason.

☑   The father acknowledges his paternity in writing.

☑   The father's paternity is established by a Court either before or after his death (FS 732.108).

If the decedent denied he was the child's father, it will take a Court procedure to establish (or disprove) paternity.

THE AFTERBORN CHILD

Under Florida law a child conceived prior to death and born to the surviving spouse after the death, has the same right to inherit as any other natural child of the decedent (FS 732.106). The child who was born or adopted after the decedent made his Will, is entitled to receive as much as he would have inherited had the decedent died without a Will unless:

⇨   it appears from the Will that the omission was intentional - or -

⇨   he left other property to the child equal in value to the child's intestate share - or -

⇨   the decedent had another child when he signed the Will and he gave all of his property to his surviving spouse, who is also the parent of the afterborn child (FL 732.302).

THE ADOPTED CHILD

An adopted person has the same right to inherit property under Florida's Laws of Intestate Success from his adoptive parents as does a natural child. The adopted child has no right to inherit from his natural parents, or his natural kinsfolk with the exception of a child whose natural parent is married to the adoptive parent. For example, if a child loses a parent and is later adopted by a step-parent, the child has the right to inherit from his natural parents and family and from his adoptive parents and family as well.

Similarly, the adoption of a child by a close relative after the death of both his parents has no effect on the relationship between the child and the family of his deceased parents (FS 732.108).

WHO DIED FIRST?

Sometimes it happens that two family members die simultaneously, and no one knows who died first. For example, suppose a husband and wife die together in a car crash, how is the property distributed in that case? Florida statute (FS 732.601) provides for an orderly distribution of their respective Estates.

In general, the property of each person is distributed as if that person survived the death of the other. For example, if the husband was insured, with his wife as the beneficiary of his life insurance policy, the proceeds of the policy will be distributed as if the wife died before her husband. The proceeds will be given to the alternate beneficiary named in the policy. If no alternate beneficiary was named, the proceeds of the policy will go to the Estate of the insured party (in this case, the husband).

JOINTLY OWNED PROPERTY

Property owned jointly by the couple, with no provision for who is to inherit the property should they both die, is divided with half going to the Estate of the husband and the other half to the Estate of the wife. If they each have a Will, the husband's half is distributed according to his Will and the wife's half according to her Will. If either dies without a Will, that half is distributed according to Florida's Laws of Intestate Succession.

HOW TO READ THE WILL

If the decedent left a Will, then the Will states who is to receive the property. Most Wills are short and easy to read; however, you may come across an unfamiliar legal term such as the term *per capita*, for example:

"I leave the rest, residue and remainder of my
property to my children, Robert, Barry and Carl,
in equal shares, per capita."

This means that if one child dies before the decedent, then the share intended for that child is to be divided equally between the surviving brothers. This is different than *per stirpes.* If the gift were left to them, in equal shares, per stirpes, and one of them died, the share would go to the children of the deceased child and not to his brothers.

Sometimes a Will is ambiguous and can be read in different ways. In such case, it may be necessary to have the Probate Court decide what the decedent intended.

In the next section, we examine different problems that can arise with the Will and when to challenge the validity of the Will.

It is not uncommon for a family member to be unhappy with the way the decedent willed his property. If you are tempted to challenge a Will, first consider whether the Will is valid under Florida law. In Florida, a Will is presumed valid if at the time the decedent made the Will he was at least 18, and of sound mind (FS 732.501).

Courts have ruled that "Sound mind" means that when the decedent made the Will he knew:

☑ what property he owned - and -

☑ who of his relatives would, under ordinary circumstances, expect to inherit his property - and -

☑ he understood the practical effect of the Will, i.e. who would inherit his property under that Will. (*American Red Cross v. Estate of Haynsworth*, 708 So.2d 602 (Fla. 1998)).

☒   THE UNWITNESSED WILL

The first step in the Probate procedure is to have the Probate court determine whether the Will presented is valid. If the Will is in writing and signed by the Will maker in the presence of at least two credible witnesses, then there should be no problem in having the Will accepted into Probate. But suppose the decedent wrote out a Will in his own hand and signed it with no one present? A Will written in the Will maker's hand is called a *holographic Will*. Florida law requires that a Will be in writing and signed in the presence of two witness, so the Probate Court will not accept an unwitnessed holographic Will into Probate (FS 732.502).

Not all states refuse to recognize a holographic Will. If the decedent died in Florida but his primary residence was in another state, you need to check whether the Probate court of that state might decide that the Will is valid.

The problem with a holographic Will, in this or any other state, is its authenticity. Because no one saw the decedent sign the Will, it is hard to determine whether the Will was written by the decedent or is a forgery. If all the decedent left was a holographic Will, then you should consult with an attorney experienced in Probate matters.

☒   UNDUE INFLUENCE

Under Florida law, a beneficiary of the Will can serve as a witness (FS 732.504). But the problem of having a beneficiary present when the Will was signed is that of *undue influence*. Undue influence occurs whenever someone exerts such pressure on the Will maker so that he is not acting according to his own free will. But undue influence is not easily proven. Florida courts have ruled that to prove undue influence, whoever challenges the Will must prove:

⇨   the person who used such pressure was a substantial beneficiary of the Will - and -

⇨   he had a close and confidential relationship with the Will maker - and -

⇨   he was instrumental in having the Will prepared; i.e., the Will was prepared because of his efforts.

If it is proved that the gift was obtained because of undue influence, the Court will consider the gift to be invalid; i.e., the person who used undue influence will not receive that gift (FS 732.5165).

☒   THE VERBAL WILL

Picture a death bed scene. The elderly gentleman is surrounded by several family members. In a whisper, just audible enough to be heard, he says: "Even though I am a wealthy man, I never got around to making a Will. You all have been good to me, but I did want my entire fortune to go to my nephew, Robert. He has been like a son to me. "

Do you think Robert can inherit his Uncle's Estate?
Not in Florida unless:

⇨   Someone writes down his uncles's wishes, and

⇨   The uncle acknowledges that this is his Will, and

⇨   The uncle either signs the Will or has someone sign it for him, and

⇨   Two people sign the Will as witnesses in the Uncle's presence and in the presence of each other (FS 732.502).

Considering that the uncle's relatives will probably inherit the fortune under the Florida's Laws of Intestate Succession, it is doubtful that Robert is in danger of becoming wealthy at any time in the near future.

⊠ THE WILL THAT IS CONTRARY TO LAW

Sometimes a person who is of sound mind, makes a Will, but that Will has the effect of giving a spouse or a minor child less than is required under Florida law. One such example is that of Nancy. Hers was not an easy life. She worked long hours as a waitress. She divorced her hard drinking first husband. The final judgment gave her their homestead, some securities, and sole custody of their son. After the divorce Nancy had her attorney prepare a Will leaving all she owned to her son, Richard.

Some years later she met and married Harry, a chef at the restaurant where she worked. He moved into her home and they later had a daughter. Richard was 19, and his stepsister 12, when Nancy died after a lengthy battle with cancer.

Nancy did not leave much — her home, and securities worth about $50,000, which were in Nancy's name only. Before she died, she told Richard, that she had not changed her Will because she wanted him to have all she owned. She said Harry had a good job and she was sure he would take good care of his daughter.

No sooner was the funeral over, when stepson came in and demanded that Harry vacate his mother's home. Harry was furious and went to his attorney.

"I was a good husband to Nancy, supporting and taking care of her all during her illness. It was me, and not her son, who was at her side when she died. Now he is telling me to get out of the house. Does he have the right to put me out?"

The attorney reassured him. "No. Under Florida law, you have the right to live in the house for the rest of your life. When you die it will be inherited by your stepson and daughter. In addition to the Life Estate in your wife's home, you can ask the Court to award you an *Elective Share*. Under Florida law, you are entitled to 30% of her Estate unless you gave up those rights by signing a pre-nuptial or post-nuptial agreement (FS 732.401)."

"No, I never signed anything. What about my daughter? Does she have any rights?"

The attorney explained "Yes. Your daughter was born after your wife made her Will. Under Florida law, if Nancy was without children at the time she made her Will, then your daughter has the right to inherit as much as she would have inherited had her mother died without a Will, unless Nancy made some other provision (FS 732.302)."

"No, she left nothing to her daughter."

Richard did not fare as well as his mother intended. The judge awarded a Family Allowance for the daughter's support while the Estate was being probated. The securities had to be sold to pay for the funeral expenses, medical bills, the Family Allowance, and the costs of probating the Estate.

All that Richard inherited was his half of the house, and he would have to wait until his stepfather died before he could take his inheritance.

No doubt Nancy did not understand what would happen to her Estate once she passed on. The Will she left did not accomplish her goal of providing for her son. All it did was /cause turmoil and an irreparable rift between Harry and Richard.

It didn't need to be that way. Had Nancy known about Florida law, she could have consulted with an attorney and set up an Estate Plan that could have provided for her son without alienating her husband.

But, the moral of the story, for the purpose of this discussion, is that if you believe that the decedent's Will is not valid or is not drafted according to Florida law, you need to consult with an attorney experienced in Probate matters to determine your legal rights under that Will.

Getting Possession Of The Property 6

Knowing who is entitled to receive the decedent's property is one thing. Getting that property is another. As explained in the previous chapter if the decedent held property jointly with someone, or in a Trust for someone, the property now belongs to the joint owner or beneficiary. If it is personal property such as a bank account or a security, the beneficiary can usually get possession of the property by giving a certified copy of the death certificate to the financial institution.

If the decedent had real or personal property in his name only, or if he held property as a Tenant In Common, then some sort of Probate proceeding may be necessary in order to transfer ownership to the proper beneficiary. The assistance of an attorney may be required should a full Probate proceeding be necessary, but there are many items that can be transferred without legal assistance. This chapter explains how to get possession of those items.

The chapter also contains an explanation of the different kinds of Probate procedures that are available in Florida, and when it is appropriate to use that procedure.

DISTRIBUTING PERSONAL EFFECTS

Too often, the first person to discover the body will help himself to the decedent's *personal effects* (clothing, jewelry, appliances, electrical equipment, cameras, books, stamp or coin collection, household items and furnishing, etc.). Unless that person is the decedent's sole beneficiary, such action is unconscionable, if not illegal.

The decedent may have left a writing, separate from his Will, making a gift of his *tangible personal property* (clothing, jewelry, etc.) but not money gifts or securities. To be distributed as part of a Probate proceeding, the writing needs to be in the decedent's own hand or if the gift was made by means of a typewritten statement, then the decedent's signature needs to appear at the end of the document (FL 732.515). If no Probate proceeding is necessary, the item can just be given to the beneficiary.

The rest of the decedent's personal effects should be given to the person appointed as the Personal Representative to be distributed according to the decedent's Will, or separate writing, or if no Will, according to the Florida Laws of Intestate Succession.

If no Probate e proceeding is necessary, the decedent's next of kin, as determined by the Laws of Intestate Succession, need to divide all of the personal effects among themselves in approximately equal proportions.

What's Equal?

The decedent's Will may direct that the decedent's personal property be divided equally between two or more beneficiaries. The problem with the term "equal" is that people have different ideas of what "equal" means. Unless there is clear evidence that the decedent's Will meant something else, "equal" refers to the monetary value of the item and not to the number of items received. For example, to divide the decedent's personal effects equally, one beneficiary may receive an expensive item of jewelry and another beneficiary may receive several items whose overall value is approximately equal to that single piece of jewelry.

When distributing personal effects there needs to be cooperation and perhaps compromise, or else bitter arguments might arise over items of little monetary value. One such argument occurred when an elderly woman died who was rich only in her love for her five children and nine grandchildren. After the funeral, the children gathered in their mother's apartment. Each child had his own furnishings and no need for anything in the apartment. They agreed to donate all of their mother's personal effects to a local charity with the exception of a few items of sentimental value.

Each child took some small item as a remembrance — a handkerchief, a large platter that their mother used to serve family dinners, a doily their mother crocheted. Things went smoothly until it came to her photograph album. Frank, the youngest sibling, said, "I'll take this." Marie objected saying "But there are pictures in that album that I want."

Frank retorted, "You already took all the pictures Mom had on her dresser."

The argument went downhill from there. Unsettled sibling rivalries boiled over, fueled by the hurt of the loss that they were all experiencing. It almost came to blows when the eldest settled the argument: "Frank you make copies of all of the photos in the album for Marie. Marie, you make copies of all of the pictures that you took and give them to Frank. This way you both will have a complete set of Mom's pictures. And while you're at it, make copies for the rest of us."

NON-PROBATE TRANSFERS

A *Non-probate transfer* is a transfer of the decedent's property without the need for Probate. For example, if the decedent had a bank account in his name only "In Trust For" someone or with instructions to "Pay On Death" to a someone, all the beneficiary need do is produce a death certificate and proper identification, and the bank will turn over the property to the beneficiary. Securities that are held jointly with someone, or with instructions to "Transfer On Death" to a named beneficiary, can be transferred to that beneficiary in the same manner.

No Probate proceeding is necessary if title to the decedent's car was held jointly with another. The surviving joint owner can go to the nearest Department of Highway Safety and Motor Vehicles office and transfer the car to his name only. He can do this on his signature alone, provided there is no lien on the car. If monies are owed on the car, title to the car cannot be changed until the lien is released. Before going to the Department of Motor Vehicles you may want to call them at (850) 922-9000 for information about the cost of the transfer and what documents they require.

TRANSFERRING THE CAR

It is a good idea to limit the use of the car until it is sold or transferred to the beneficiary. If the decedent's car is involved in an accident before the car is transferred to the new owner, the decedent's Estate may be liable for the damage. Having adequate insurance on the car may save the Estate from monetary loss, but a pending lawsuit could delay Probate and prevent any money from being distributed to the beneficiaries until the lawsuit is settled.

If Probate is necessary, it is the job of the Personal Representative to transfer the decedent's car to the proper beneficiary. The surviving spouse has the right to the decedent's car as Exempt Property (page 101). If the surviving spouse does not want the car, or if the decedent was single, the Personal Representative with transfer the car according to the terms of the Will.

If the Will makes a *specific gift* of the car, the Personal Representative will transfer the car to that person. If there was no mention of the car in the decedent's Will, it goes to the *residuary beneficiaries* under the Will, i.e., those who inherit whatever is left once all the bills have been paid and all the special gifts made in the Will are distributed. If the decedent did not have a Will, the car goes to the decedent's heirs as determined by Florida's Laws of Intestate Succession.

If the car was owned in the decedent's name only, and Probate is not necessary, the Department of Highway Safety and Motor Vehicles will issue new title to the proper beneficiary provided there is no outstanding debt on the car; and all those who have a right to inherit the vehicle agree to the transfer (FS 319.28).

If you are the beneficiary of the car and are going to keep it for your own use, you will also need to register it in your name and purchase a new set of license plates.

TRANSFER WHEN MORE THAN ONE BENEFICIARY

If more than one person who has the right to inherit the car, they all can take title to the car. That may not be a practical thing to do since only one person can drive the car at any given time and if one gets into an accident, they all can be held liable. The better route is for the beneficiaries to agree to have one person take title to the car. The person taking title will need to compensate the others for their share of the car. In such case the bene-ficiaries need to come to an agreement as to the value of the car.

DETERMINING THE VALUE OF THE CAR

Cars are valued in different ways. The *collateral* value of the car is the value that banks use to evaluate the car for purposes of making a loan to the owner of the car. If you were to trade in a car for the purpose of purchasing a new one, the car dealer would offer you its *wholesale* value. Were you to purchase that same car from a car dealer, he would price it at its *retail* or *fair market value*. Usually the retail price is highest, wholesale is lowest and its collateral value is somewhere in between.

You can call your local bank to get the collateral value of the car. It may be more difficult to obtain the wholesale value because the amount of money a dealer is willing to pay depends on the value of the new car that you are purchasing. You can determine the car's retail value by looking at comparable used car advertisements in the local newspaper.

Rather than going through the effort of determining these three values, you can use your Internet search engine to look up the Kelly Blue Book Value. This publication gives Low, Average and High Blue Book Values which correspond to the wholesale, collateral and retail values. Once the fair market value of the car is determined, the transfer can be made.

Regardless of the value of the car, the Department of Highway Safety and Motor Vehicles will issue new title to the new owner without the necessity of going through a Probate proceeding provided all those who have a right to inherit the vehicle agree to the transfer (FS 319.28).

Form HSMV 82040 will need to be signed by everyone who is entitled to inherit the car. By signing this release each person is giving up his right to the car to the person identified on the form as the "Applicant." You can download the form from the Department Web site.
http://www.hsmv.state.fl.us

Each person who signs Form HSMV 82040, must certify that:

> ➢ the Estate is not indebted, and
> ➢ there are sufficient assets to pay any just claim against the Estate, and
> ➢ there is no ongoing Probate.

If you are a beneficiary of the car, you should not sign this form if any of these statements are not true, but instead consult with an attorney to assist in clearing up the problem.

The leased car is not an asset of the Estate because the decedent did not own the car. The leased car is a liability to the Estate because the decedent was obligated to pay the balance of the monies owed on the lease agreement. The Personal Representative, or next of kin, need to work out an agreement with the company to either assign the lease to a beneficiary or family member who will agree to pay for the lease — or to have the Estate pay off the lease by purchasing the car under the terms of the lease agreement.

Some lenders will allow the lease to be assigned to a beneficiary provided the Estate remains liable for the balance of payment. In such cases, it is better to have the beneficiary refinance the car and have the original lease agreement paid in full.

If the remaining payments exceed the current market value of the car, there may be a temptation to hand the keys over to the leasing company. This may not be the best strategy, because the leasing company can sell the car and then sue the Estate for the balance of the monies owed. If the decedent had no assets or if the only assets he had are creditor proof, then simply returning the car may be an option. But if the decedent's Estate has assets available to pay the balance of the lease payments, then the Personal Representative needs to arrange to have the car transferred in a way that releases the Estate from all further liability.

TRANSFERRING THE MOBILE HOME

A mobile home is transferred the same as any other motor vehicle. Before transferring the motor vehicle, you need to find out whether the land on which the mobile home is located was leased or owned by the decedent. If the decedent was renting space in a trailer park, you need to contact the trailer park owner to transfer the lease agreement to the beneficiary of the mobile home. If the decedent owned the land under the mobile home, then a Probate proceeding will be necessary to transfer the land to the proper beneficiary. The transfer of real property is discussed later in this Chapter.

TRANSFERRING WATERCRAFT

Motor boats are transferred in the same manner as any other motor vehicle. If no Probate proceeding is necessary, the boat can be transferred without going through a Probate procedure (FS 319.28). If a Probate proceeding is necessary, the Personal Representative is responsible to transfer the boat. When the ownership of a registered vessel changes, the new owner needs to file an application for transfer of title and registration with the County Tax Collector (FS 328.03, 328.72).

TRANSFERRING AIRCRAFT

The Florida Department of Transportation does not register aircraft, but they do require that any aircraft operated within the state be registered with Federal Aviation Administration ("FAA") (FS 329.01, 329.10). See page 69 for information about contacting the FAA to change title and registration of the aircraft.

THE INCOME TAX REFUND

Any refund due to the decedent under a joint federal income tax return filed by his surviving spouse will be sent to the surviving spouse. If the decedent's Personal Representative filed the final return, the refund check will be sent to him to be deposited to the Estate account.

If the decedent was single and no Probate proceeding is necessary, under Florida law, an IRS refund of $2,500 or less, goes to the decedent's child. If the decedent had more than one child, all of the children over the age of 14 need to agree to have the money distributed to one of the children (FS 735.302).

To receive the refund the child must sign an Affidavit stating that:

➢ no one has started a Probate proceeding and none is planned AND

➢ the decedent was not indebted, or if indebted, arrangements have been made to pay the debt, or the Estate is exempt from the claims of creditors under Florida law.

If the refund is greater than $2,500, or if the decedent was single without children, a Probate proceeding will be necessary to determine who is entitled to the check.

The refund can be obtained by filing IRS form 1310 along with the decedent's final income tax return (the 1040). You can obtain form 1310 by calling the IRS at (800) 829-3676. You can download forms, instructions and publications from the Internal Revenue Service by going to the **FORMS AND PUBLICATIONS** section of their Web site.

 INTERNAL REVENUE SERVICE
http://www.irs.gov/

THE SMALL ESTATE PROCEDURE

There is no need to go through a full Probate proceeding if the decedent left only personal property that is exempt from his creditors (see page 102) and non-exempt personal property worth less than the cost of the decedent's "preferred" funeral expenses and final medical bills (FS 735.301).

As explained in Chapter 4, there is a priority of payment. The decedent's funeral, burial and grave marker expenses are second in priority but only up to $6,000. Anything over $6,000 becomes a Class 8 debt. The word "preferred" is not defined in Florida Statute 735.301; however, we assume that the statute refers to funeral expenses up to $6,000.

Florida Statute 733.707 limits the decedent's final medical expenses to those "... reasonable and necessary medical and hospital expenses of the last 60 days of the illness." The statute does not limit the medical expenses to those not covered by insurance, but the intent seems to be to reimburse the family for monies they paid, out of pocket, for the care and burial of the decedent.

If you believe the statute applies in your case, you need to apply to the Clerk of the Circuit Court in the Probate Division of the county where the decedent lived. If the decedent had a Will, you need to file the original Will with the Probate Clerk, if you have not already done so. You also need to file a certified copy of the death certificate and pay a filing fee. The current (2005) fee for filing A DISPOSITION OF PERSONAL PROPERTY WITHOUT ADMINIS-TRATION is $102.

The judge needs to be satisfied that you qualify under that statute and that everything you say is true. The best way to demonstrate to the judge that you are telling the truth is to sign an *Affidavit* stating the facts of the case and attaching documents to the Affidavit to back up each fact.

An Affidavit is a written statement in which the *Affiant* (the person signing the statement) swears, under oath, that each fact in the Affidavit is true. You can sign the Affidavit in the presence of the Clerk of the Circuit Court or you can sign it in the presence of a notary public before you go to court.

If the judge is satisfied that you meet the criteria for Florida Statute 735.301, he will issue a letter or other writing that authorizes the payment or transfer of the decedent's property to the proper beneficiary. You can take that letter or document to the bank, or other person or company who has possession of the decedent's property and they should transfer his property to you.

THE SUMMARY ADMINISTRATION

A *Summary Administration* is a shortened Probate procedure. In Florida, Summary Administration is available if:
⇨ the decedent's Estate (not counting the value of Exempt Property) does not exceed $75,000
- or -
⇨ the decedent has been dead for more than two years.

A Petition for Summary Administration must be filed with the Probate Court. The Petition asks the Court for an Order directing the transfer of the decedent's property to the proper beneficiary. If there is a Will, it must be admitted to Probate; i.e., the judge must be satisfied that it is a valid Will. Summary Administration is not available if the Will requires a full Probate procedure. The judge will want to be assured that the decedent's creditors have had an opportunity to file a claim against the Estate. That means he will want to have a Notice of Administration published in the newspaper.

Although Florida law allows the beneficiaries of the Estate to file the Petition without the assistance of a lawyer, few people have the legal skills necessary to obtain the Order. And Summary Administration is not available if:
☒ someone challenges the Will
☒ there is a dispute about who has the right to inherit the Estate
☒ there is an argument about what each beneficiary should receive;
☒ there is a disagreement about whether a bill should be paid
☒ there is not enough money in the Estate to pay all valid claims (FS 735.201, 735.203).
Should any of these issues arise, there will need to be a full Probate procedure.

No Probate procedure is necessary to transfer real property if the decedent held that property:

⇨   as the owner of a Life Estate - or -

⇨   Jointly with Right of Survivorship - or -

⇨   as Tenants by the Entirety (i.e., as husband and wife).

The survivor joint owner(s) or the remainder beneficiary of the Life Estate owns the property as of the date of death, however, the decedent's name remains on the deed. Anyone examining title to the property will not know of the death. The Bureau of Vital Statistics is responsible to issue the death certificate, but not to publish it or make it part of the public record. Of course, if there is a Probate proceeding, anyone can look up those public records and learn of the death. If no Probate is necessary and you are the surviving owner, you can go to the Clerk of the Circuit Court in the Recording Division in the county where the property is located and have the death certificate recorded. The Clerk will record a certified copy of the death certificate that does not state the cause of death (see Page 27).

Once the death certificate is recorded, any one who examines the county record will know of the death of the decedent and that the surviving owners now have full authority to occupy or transfer the property.

If the decedent held real property in his name only or as a Tenant In Common, then a Probate proceeding is necessary. The attorney for the Personal Representative will prepare and record a **Deed of Distribution** transferring the property to the proper beneficiary. If you are the beneficiary of that property, you should receive the original recorded Deed of Distribution for your records.

Each state regulates the transfer of real property within that state. Many states, like Florida, do not require that any document be recorded to transfer real property to a joint tenant who has a Right of Survivorship, or to a remainder beneficiary of a Life Estate interest. All the Grantee need do is keep a certified copy of the death certificate available to produce at closing when the property is transferred.

Some states, including Florida, allow the death certificate to be recorded in the county where the property is located, so that anyone examining title to the property will know who now owns the property. In other states, an Affidavit of Survivorship is recorded along with the death certificate. If the decedent owned out of state real property jointly with Rights of Survivorship, or if he held a Life Estate interest, you may want to call the recording department in the county where the property is located to find out what documents (if any) need to be recorded to let people know that the surviving Grantee now owns the property. In Florida, the Clerk of the Circuit Court is in charge of recording deeds. In other states, it might be the County Registrar or the County Recorder.

Of course, if the decedent owned real property in his name only or as a Tenant In Common, you need to contact an attorney in that state to have the property transferred to the proper beneficiary.

THE FULL PROBATE PROCEDURE

There needs to be a full Probate proceeding if the decedent left real property in his name only or as a Tenant-In-Common; or if he left personal property worth more than $10,000. The proceeding can take anywhere from several months to more than a year depending on the size and complexity of the Probate Estate. A Personal Representative must be appointed and Letters issued.

APPOINTING THE PERSONAL REPRESENTATIVE

Florida statute gives an order of priority in the appointment of a Personal Representative. Whoever the decedent named as Personal Representative or Executor of his Will has top priority. If that person is unable or unwilling to serve, the person named as Successor Personal Representative has priority. If neither of these are willing or able to serve, the beneficiaries can, by majority vote, choose a Personal Representative.

If the decedent died without a Will, the surviving spouse has the right to be Personal Representative. If the spouse is unable or unwilling to serve, or if the decedent was single, those who are entitled to inherit his Estate can elect a Personal Representative by majority vote (FS 733.301).

Whoever wishes to serve as Personal Representative must be at least 18 years of age and never have been convicted of a felony. A person who does not live in Florida can serve as Personal Representative, but only if he is related to the decedent through blood or marriage.

YOUR RIGHTS AS A BENEFICIARY

The Personal Representative is in charge of settling the Estate. Too often, beneficiaries of the Estate have no idea of what is going on. They wait to receive their inheritance, not knowing that they have rights under Florida law; and more importantly, not knowing how to assert their rights.

✧   RIGHT TO RECEIVE NOTICE

The Personal Representative is required to give notice that he is administering the Estate to the following people:
⇨   the surviving spouse
⇨   any beneficiary of the Estate
⇨   if the decedent had a Trust, then to the Trustee of the Trust
⇨   anyone who may be entitled to Exempt Property (see page 102).

The notice will give the name and address of the Personal Representative and that of his attorney. It will also say whether there was a Will and that anyone who wants to challenge the appointment of the Personal Representative or the validity of the Will must do so within three months of receiving such notice (FS 733.212). If you object to him serving as Personal Representative or you want to challenge the Will, you need to promptly let the court know of your concerns. You can do this on your own, however, it is best to consult with an attorney.

✧   RIGHT TO YOUR OWN ATTORNEY

The attorney who handles the Estate is employed by, and represents, the Personal Representative. If the Estate is sizeable, then you might consider employing your own attorney to check that things are done properly and in a timely manner. Even if the Estate is small, consider consulting with an attorney any time you are concerned about the way the Probate is being conducted.

✧ RIGHT TO APPEAR BEFORE THE COURT

Should a problem arise, you have the right to go before the Court on your own but before doing so, you should consult with an experienced Probate attorney. He can explain the best way for you to present your concerns to the Court. He can tell you what arguments have a good chance of swaying the Judge. And he can tell you which arguments have so little probability of success that they are not worth pursuing.

✧ RIGHT TO HAVE ASSETS PROTECTED

It doesn't happen often, but every now and again a Personal Representative will run off with Estate funds. A bond is insurance for the Estate. If Estate monies are stolen the company that issued the bond will reimburse the Estate for the loss. Most Wills state that no bond shall be required. The reason is two-fold. The Will maker chooses someone he trusts to administer the Estate, so he does not think a bond is necessary. And there are economic reasons. The cost of the bond is paid for by the Estate, and ultimately the amount inherited is reduced by the amount paid for the bond.

Regardless of what the Will says, the judge will decide whether a bond is necessary, and if so, the value of the bond. In most cases, he will order a bond equal to the liquid assets of the Estate; i.e., property that can easily be converted to cash. The Court will not order a bond if the Personal Representative is an authorized bank or trust company (FS 733.402, 733.403).

✧ RIGHT TO KNOW PERSONAL REPRESENTATIVE'S FEES

The Personal Representative is entitled to be compensated for his efforts in settling the Estate. If he is also a beneficiary of the Estate he may decide not to take a commission and just take his inheritance. The reason may be economic. Any fee the Representative takes is taxable as ordinary income, but monies inherited are not taxable to him as a beneficiary. Ask the Personal Representative to tell you, in writing, whether he intends to charge a fee, and if so, how much.

There are statutory guidelines for what is "reasonable" compensation in the state of Florida. The Personal Representative is entitled to:

3% of the first million dollars

2.5% of amounts over $1,000,000 and up to $5,000,000

2% of amounts over $5,000,000 and up to $10,000

1.5% of amounts over ten million dollars.

Compensation for the Personal Representative is subject to the Court's approval. When awarding fees the Court can take into account extraordinary or unusual services performed by the Personal Representative. For example, additional compensation can be awarded for:

⇨ selling real or personal property

⇨ participating in a proceeding involving the adjustment of Estate Taxes

⇨ conducting a law suit on behalf of or against the decedent's Estate

⇨ carrying on the decedent's business (FS 733.617)

✧ RIGHT TO KNOW THE ATTORNEY'S FEES

It is the Personal Representative's job to use the Probate Estate to pay all valid claims and then to distribute what is left to the proper beneficiary. Debts are paid from the decedent's Estate and not from the Representative's pocket; but if the Personal Representative makes a mistake, he may be responsible to pay for it. For example, if he pays a debt that did not need to be paid — or if he transfers property to the beneficiaries too quickly and there were still taxes due on the Estate, he may be responsible to pay for the error (FS 198.23).

The Personal Representative has the right to employ an attorney to guide him through the Probate procedure so that things will be done properly and at no personal cost to him. It is proper to have the attorney paid with Estate funds. You, as a beneficiary of the Estate, have the right to know how much will be charged for legal fees. Ask the Personal Representative to give you a copy of the retainer agreement. If the attorney is employed on an hourly basis, have the attorney give a written estimate of the time he expects to spend on the Probate proceeding. As with Personal Representative's fees, there are statutory guidelines for what is "reasonable" compensation. Florida statute 733.6171 contains a schedule of attorney's fees. It is based on the value of the Probate Estate.

$1,500 for Estates of $40,000 or less   - plus -
  $750 for Estates greater than $40,000
          but less than $70,000   - plus -
  $750 for Estates greater than $70,000
          but less than $100,000   - plus -
     3% on the next $900,000, then
2.5% of amounts above 1 million but less than 3 million
2% of amounts over 3 million but less than 5 million
1.5% of amounts over 5 million but less than 10 million
1% of amounts over 10 million dollars

If the attorney prepares the federal Estate Tax return, the attorney is entitled to percentage of the value of the gross Estate, which according to the statue is:

0.5% for Estates up to 10 million dollars - plus -
0.25% of amounts over 10 million dollars.

The above fee schedule is for "ordinary" services. The attorney is entitled to additional compensation for any "extraordinary" service. Florida statute 733.6171 lists 11 items in addition to preparing the federal Estate Tax return. The list includes disputes of any kind (Will disputes, fees disputes, claim disputes, etc.). The sale, lease or purchase of real property, legal advice relating to the continuation of the decedent's business during the Probate procedure and any kind of tax advice, are also considered "extraordinary" services, that may entitle the attorney to additional compensation.

The statutory values for Personal Representative and attorney fees are significant. Even for an Estate as small as $75,000, the Personal Representative's fee is $2,250 and his attorney's fee is $3,000. But as with most business matters, prices are negotiable. If the beneficiaries have the right to choose a Personal Representative, they should come to a fee agreement before voting for that person.

Whoever is going to be Personal Representative has the right to choose the lawyer for the Probate. The statutory fees are guidelines only. The Personal Representative can negotiate with the attorney for a lesser value. In most areas of the nation, there is sufficient competition in the legal profession so that the Personal Representative can comparison shop and negotiate the best price.

✧ RIGHT TO COPY OF INVENTORY

The Personal Representative must prepare an inventory of all of the assets of the Probate Estate within 60 days of his appointment and file it with the Court. He is required to send a copy of the inventory to the beneficiaries of the Estate and to any interested party who asks for a copy (FS 733.604). The value of the inventory may be used to determine the fees for the Personal Representative and his attorney. It is also the value used to determine whether Estate Taxes are due. It is important that you receive a copy of the inventory, and that you are satisfied with the value assigned to each item.

✧ RIGHT TO AN APPRAISAL

The Personal Representative can employ an appraiser to assist in determining the value of items included in the Estate inventory — but he is not required to have an appraisal unless ordered by the Court. If you are not satisfied with the value assigned to any Probate asset, you have the right to ask the Personal Representative to have the item appraised. If he refuses, you can ask the Court to order an independent appraisal of the item.

✧ RIGHT TO AN ACCOUNTING

Before the Estate is closed, the Personal Representative must give each residuary beneficiary an accounting, starting with the inventory value of the Estate and ending with the amount of money that will be left to distribute after all the bills have been paid. The Court will not require an accounting if all of the beneficiaries sign a waiver giving up their right to an accounting. But it is important that you review how the Estate monies were spent. If you do not do so, once the Court discharges the Personal Representative, it will be difficult, if not impossible to hold him accountable for losses to the Estate (FS 733.901).

✧ RIGHT TO HAVE THE ESTATE CLOSED WITHOUT DELAY

How long it takes to complete the Probate proceeding depends on the size and complexity of the matter. The Personal Representative is not required to make any distribution to a beneficiary until creditors have had an opportunity to come forward and file their claims — that's usually five months from his appointment (FS 733.801).

Unless there is some unusual circumstance, such as a Court battle over some part of the Probate proceeding, the Estate should be closed within one year from the publication of the Notice To Creditors. If an Estate Tax return has been filed, the Estate should be closed within 90 days after the receipt of federal and state tax releases. If you do not receive an accounting and a proposed plan of distributing funds to the beneficiaries within these time periods, you have the right to ask the Court to order the Personal Representative do an accounting.

✧ RIGHT TO RECEIVE A DEBT FREE INHERITANCE

Once a beneficiary finally receives his inheritance, about the last thing he wants to hear is that there is some unfinished business, or worse yet that monies need to be paid from the inheritance he received. But that is just what could happen if the Personal Representative distributes the money before all the creditors are paid.

Taxes are another concern. You should ask to see a copy of all of the tax returns that were filed, and then verify that any monies that were due have been paid. Most importantly, you should not agree to having the Estate closed if the closing statement shows that there are any outstanding debts that need to be paid.

IT'S YOUR RIGHT - DON'T BE INTIMIDATED

You may feel uncomfortable being assertive with a friend or family member who is Personal Representative. Don't be. It's your money and your right to be informed. Be especially firm if the Personal Representative waves you off with "You've known me for years. Surely you trust me." People who are trustworthy don't ask to be trusted. They do what is right. The very fact that the Personal Representative is resisting, is a red flag. In such situation, you can explain that it is not a matter of trust, but a matter of what is your legal right.

At the same time, keep things in perspective. Your relationship with the Personal Representative may be more important to you than the money you inherit. The job of settling an Estate can be complex and demanding. If the Personal Representative is getting the job done, let him know you appreciate his efforts.

THE CHECK LIST

We have discussed many things that need to be done when someone dies in the state of Florida. The next page contains a check list that you may find helpful.

You can check those items that you need to do, and then cross them off the list once they are done. We made the list as comprehensive as possible, so many items may not apply in your case. In such case, you can cross them off the list or mark them *N/A* (not applicable).

Things To Do

FUNERAL ARRANGEMENTS TO BE MADE

☐ AUTOPSY   ☐ ANATOMICAL GIFT

☐ DISPOSITION OF BODY OR ASHES

DEATH CERTIFICATE

☐ HAVE CERTIFICATE RECORDED

GIVE COPY TO: _____

_____

NOTICE OF DEATH

PEOPLE TO BE NOTIFIED _____

COMPANIES TO NOTIFY

☐ TELEPHONE COMPANY

    ☐ LOCAL COMPANY ☐ LONG DISTANCE ☐ CELLULAR

☐ NEWSPAPER (OBITUARY PRINTED)

☐ NEWSPAPER DELIVERY CANCELLED   ☐ deposit refund

☐ SOCIAL SECURITY

☐ INTERNET SERVER CANCELLED

☐ TELEVISION CABLE/SATELLITE COMPANY CANCELLED

☐ POWER & LIGHT   ☐ deposit refund

☐ POST OFFICE

☐ OTHER UTILITIES (GAS, WATER)   ☐ deposit refund

☐ PENSION PLAN

☐ ANNUITY

☐ HEALTH INSURANCE COMPANY

☐ LIFE INSURANCE COMPANY

☐ HOME INSURANCE COMPANY

☐ MOTOR VEHICLE INSURANCE COMPANY

☐ CONDOMINIUM OR HOMEOWNER ASSOCIATION

☐ CANCEL SERVICE CONTRACT   ☐ deposit refund

☐ CREDIT CARD COMPANIES

_____

_____

_____

Things To Do

REMOVE DECEDENT AS BENEFICIARY OF:
- ☐ WILL ☐ INSURANCE POLICY ☐ PENSION PLAN
- ☐ BANK OR IRA ACCOUNT ☐ SECURITY

DEBTS
PAY DECEDENT'S DEBTS (AMOUNT & CREDITOR)

_____

COLLECT MONIES OWED TO DECEDENT (AMOUNT & DEBTOR)

_____

TAXES
- ☐ FILE FINAL FEDERAL INCOME TAX RETURN
- ☐ RECEIVE INCOME TAX REFUND
- ☐ FILE ESTATE TAX RETURN

PROPERTY TO BE TRANSFERRED
- ☐ PERSONAL EFFECTS
- ☐ MOTOR VEHICLE
- ☐ BANK ACCOUNT
- ☐ CREDIT UNION ACCOUNT
- ☐ IRA ACCOUNT
- ☐ SECURITIES
- ☐ BROKERAGE ACCOUNT
- ☐ INSURANCE PROCEEDS
- ☐ HOMESTEAD
- ☐ TIME SHARE
- ☐ OTHER REAL PROPERTY
- ☐ CONTENTS OF SAFE DEPOSIT BOX

OTHER THINGS TO DO

_____
_____
_____

Once the Probate proceeding is over, you will be left with many documents and wonder which you need to keep:

COURT DOCUMENTS

You should keep a copy of the inventory to establish the value of property that you inherit. That value becomes your basis for any Capital Gains Tax that you may need to pay in the future. Other than the inventory, there is no reason to keep any Court document, provided you are satisfied with the way things were done; and do not intend to take action against the Personal Representative, or his attorney. The Clerk of the Probate Court keeps the Probate file on record, so if for some reason you later need a copy of a Probate document, you can get it from the Clerk.

PERSONAL RECORDS

The surviving spouse, or if no spouse, his next of kin should keep the decedent's personal papers (birth certificate, marriage certificate, naturalization papers, army records, religious documents, etc.). They may be needed in order to apply for government, or other, benefits. The next of kin may want to keep the decedent's medical records in the event that a family member needs to check out a genetic disease.

TAX RECORDS

The IRS has up to three years to collect additional taxes, and you have up to seven years to claim a loss from a worthless security, so you should keep the decedent's tax file for seven years from the date of filing the return. You can learn more about which records to keep from the IRS publication 552. You can get the publication by calling the IRS at (800) 829-3676 or you can download it / from their Web site: http://www.irs.gov

Everyman's Estate Plan 7

The first six chapters of this book describe how to wind up the affairs of the decedent. As you read those chapters, you learned about the kinds of problems that can occur when settling the decedent's Estate. It is relatively simple for you to set up an Estate Plan so that your family members are not burdened with similar problems. An *Estate Plan* is the arranging of your finances for maximum control and protection during your lifetime, and at the same time ensuring that your property will be transferred quickly and at little cost to your heirs.

If you think that only wealthy people need to prepare an Estate Plan, you are mistaken. Each year, heirs of relatively modest Estates, spend thousands of dollars to settle an Estate. A bit of planning could have eliminated most, if not all, of the expense and hassle suffered by those families.

The suggestions in this chapter are designed to assist the average person in preparing a practical and inexpensive Estate Plan, so we named this chapter EVERYMAN'S ESTATE PLAN.

Once you create your own Estate Plan, you can be assured that your family will not be left with more problems than happy memories of you.

AVOIDING PROBATE

After reading the last chapter, many will come to the conclusion that Probate is a good thing to avoid. Those Estates with less than $75,000 (and no real property) can go through a Summary Administration, but as explained in the last chapter, they will probably need the assistance of an attorney to do so, and it may cost them thousands of dollars to get possession of your property

If you who own real property, or property in excess of $75,000, that is titled in your name only, then a full Probate will be necessary with all of its inherent delays and expenses. Notice that the operative phrase in the last sentence is *in your name only.* Whether a Probate procedure is necessary depends on how your property is titled (owned). It makes no difference whether you do or do not have a Will. If you own property in your name only, your beneficiaries will probably go through a Probate to get possession of their inheritance.

As explained in Chapter 5, there are many ways to title real property so that it passes automatically without the need for Probate. For example, You can own real property Jointly with Rights of Survivorship. Upon your death, the survivors will own the property without the need to go through Probate. Similarly if you own a Life Estate, upon your death, the property passes directly to the owner of the remainder interest in the property.

In this Chapter we will examine ways to title your personal property (bank accounts, securities, etc.) so that they pass to your beneficiaries without the need for Probate.

OWNERSHIP OF BANK ACCOUNTS

You can arrange to have all of your bank accounts set up so that should you die, the money goes directly to a beneficiary. For example, suppose all you own is a bank account and you want whatever you have in the account to go to your son and daughter when you die. You might think that a simple solution is to put each child's name on the account as joint tenants with Right of Survivorship, but first consider the problems associated with a joint account.

☒ POTENTIAL LIABILITY

If you hold a bank account jointly with your adult child and that child is sued or gets a divorce, the child may need to disclose his ownership of the joint account. In such a case, you may find yourself spending money to prove that the account was established for your convenience only and that all of the money in that account really belongs to you.

☒ OVERREACHING

If you set up a joint account with your child so that the child has authority to withdraw funds from the account, monies could be withdrawn without your knowledge or consent.

If you open a multiple party account with two of your children, there is the problem of what happens to the funds after your death. Should you die, your share of the account belongs to the surviving joint owners, equally. But as a practical matter each joint owner has free access to the joint account. After your death the first child to the bank may decide to withdraw all of the money and that will, at the very least, cause hard feelings between them.

Holding a bank account jointly with a family member eliminates the need for Probate, but at the cost of control of the funds. One way to avoid Probate of the account, yet retain full control during your lifetime, is to name one or more persons to be the beneficiary of the account. There are two forms of **Beneficiary Account**. Your contract with the bank can direct the bank to hold your account **In Trust For** ("ITF") one or more beneficiaries that you name. An In Trust For account is also known as a *Totten Trust.*

Another type of beneficiary account is an account that directs the bank to **Pay On Death** ("POD") all of the money in the account to one or more beneficiaries that you name (FS 655.82, 655.825).

The contract you sign with the bank will give instructions to be followed should you die while the account is open. If you open an In Trust For or Pay On Death account, unless the contract with your bank states differently, under Florida law:

⇨   The beneficiary does not have any right (or access) to the account during your lifetime.

⇨   you are free to change beneficiaries without asking the beneficiary's permission to do so.

⇨   If you name two or more beneficiaries, the funds are divided equally between them upon your death. Unless your agreement with the bank states otherwise, if one of your beneficiary dies, the surviving beneficiary will inherit the account. (FS 655.81).

TRANSFER ON DEATH SECURITIES

The Florida law for securities is much the same as the statutes for bank accounts. You can arrange to have a security (a stock, bond or brokerage account) transferred to a beneficiary upon your death. You can instruct the holder of the security to Pay On Death ("POD") or *Transfer On Death* ("TOD") to a named beneficiary.

If the beneficiary of the security dies before you, the security will become part of your Estate. However, you can direct that if the beneficiary dies first, his descendants inherit the security. For example, a security account can be titled as: Alice Lee TOD Wayne Lee LDPS, which is short-hand for:

> Alice Lee is the owner of the securities account. Upon her death, transfer the securities in her account to Wayne Lee. If Wayne dies before Alice, give the securities to Wayne's lineal descendants, per stirpes.

The is much the same as the POD account. Wayne has no right to the securities until Alice dies. Alice is free to close the account or to change beneficiaries, without permission from Wayne (FS 711.51, 711.505, 711.506, 711.507).

If your Estate consists only of bank accounts and/or securities, and you want all of your property to go to one or two beneficiaries without the need for Probate, but with maximum control and protection of your funds during your lifetime, then holding your property in any of these beneficiary forms:

"In Trust For"
"Pay-On-Death"
"Transfer-On-Death"

should accomplish your goal.

GIFT TO A MINOR CHILD

At the beginning of this chapter, we identified two problems with a joint account: potential liability if the joint owner is sued and overreaching by the joint owner. If you wish to make a gift to a minor child, then that presents still another problem. The POD and TOD account avoids the problem of potential liability and overreaching, but if the beneficiary of such account is a minor, there is the problem of the child having access to a large sum of money.

Under Florida law, if the amount in the account is under $10,000, the financial institution can transfer the funds to whoever has custody of the child. If the amount exceeds $10,000, the company will not transfer the funds without authorization from the Probate Court (FS 710.108). The Court may decide that it is necessary to appoint a Guardian to care for the child's property.

You may think it best that the child inherits more than $10,000. This way a Court will see to it that the monies are held safely till the child is an adult. But that only presents a new set of problems. It takes time, effort and money to set up a Guardianship. If you leave the child a significant amount of money, the Guardian has the right to be paid to manage those funds. It could happen that the cost of the Guardianship significantly reduces the amount of money inherited by the child. There are ways to avoid the problem of having a Guardian appointed to care for property inherited by a child, and yet ensuring that the monies are protected. One such method is the FLORIDA UNIFORM TRANSFERS TO MINORS ACT.

THE UNIFORM TRANSFERS TO MINORS ACT

The *Florida Uniform Transfers to Minors Act* is designed to protect gifts made to a minor by appointing someone to be the *Custodian* of a gift until the child is an adult. For example, you can make a minor child the beneficiary of your life insurance policy, and name a trusted relative or friend or even a financial institution to be the Custodian of the gift. Should you die while the child is a minor, the insurance company will give the proceeds of the policy to the person you named as Custodian to hold until the child is an adult.

You can make a gift to a minor in your Will. You can appoint your Personal Representative (or anyone else) as Custodian of the gift. For example:

I give the sum of $20,000 to _____ (name) as custodian for _____(name of minor) under the Florida Uniform Transfers to Minors Act.

THE LIFETIME GIFT

You can even use the Florida Uniform Transfers to Minors Law to make a gift during your lifetime of some item such as shares in a corporation or a limited partnership interest. You can nominate yourself as Custodian of the gift, or you can name another person to serve as Custodian. Once the lifetime gift is made it becomes irrevocable, so this method is not appropriate unless you are sure that you want the child to have the gift once he is an adult.

In general, the Custodian must distribute the gift when the child reaches 18; however, if you make a lifetime gift, or a gift as part of your Will, you can direct the Custodian to distribute the gift when the child reaches 21 (FS 710.104, 710.105, 710.106, 710.108, 710.123).

The Custodian needs to invest and manage the property in a responsible, prudent manner. He must keep records of all transactions made with custodial property; and make those records available for inspection by the child's parent, or legal representative, or the child, if the minor is 14 or older. If those records are not to their satisfaction, they can petition (ask) the Probate Court to require the Custodian to give an accounting (FS 710.114).

The Custodian has the discretion to use the gift to care for the child. The Custodian can pay monies directly to the child, or can use the money for the child's benefit. The Custodian can refuse to use any of the monies for the child and just keep the funds invested until the child reaches 21. If the Custodian wants to keep the funds invested the child's parent, or his legal representative, or the child once he is 14, can ask the Judge of the Probate Court to order the Custodian to part with some or all of the money for the benefit of the child. The Judge will decide what is in the child's best interest and then rule on the matter (FS 710.116).

The Custodian is entitled to be paid for his effort each year (FS 710.117). If the gift is sizeable, the Custodian's fee can be sizeable. Before appointing a person or a financial institution as Custodian, it is best to come to a written agreement about what will be charged to manage the custodial property.

A gift made under the Florida Uniform Transfers to Minors Act is limited to one minor only (FS 710.112). If you want to give a single gift, such as a gift of real property to two or more children or if you want more flexibility about when the minor is to receive the gift, then a Trust may be the better way to go.

We will discuss Trusts later in this chapter.

THE GIFT OF REAL PROPERTY

As explained in Chapter 5, if you own real property together with another, then who owns the property upon your death depends on how the Grantee is identified on the face of the deed. If you compare the Grantee clause of the deed to the examples on pages 101 through 107 you can determine who will inherit the property should you die. If you are not satisfied with the way the property will be inherited, then you need to consult with an attorney to change the deed so that it will conform to your wishes.

If you own the property in your name only, when you die, there will need to be a Probate proceeding to determine the proper beneficiary of that parcel of land. If your main objective is to avoid Probate, you can have an attorney change the deed so that upon your death, the property will descends to your beneficiary without the need for Probate. As with bank and securities accounts there are different ways to do so, each with its own advantages and disadvantages.

JOINT OWNERSHIP

If you hold property in your name only, and wish to avoid Probate, you can have your deed changed so that you and a beneficiary are joint owners with rights of survivorship. If you do so, should either of you die, the other will own the property 100%. That avoids Probate, but by making that person joint owner, you are, in effect, making a gift of half of the property during your lifetime. You will not be able to sell that property without the beneficiary's permission. And if the beneficiary gives permission and the property is sold, the beneficiary will have the legal right to half of the proceeds of the sale. As explained on the next page, you may be creating tax problems as well.

You can arrange to sell your home without paying a Capital Gains Tax (see page 42), but if you make someone joint owner of your home who does not live with you, a Capital Gains Tax may need to be paid on the joint owner's share of the proceeds should you decide to sell the property.

 ## GIFT OF HOMESTEAD

Some elderly parents worry that they may need nursing care at some time in the future and lose all of their life savings to pay for that care. The parent may decide that the best way to avoid Probate and protect the homestead from loss is to transfer the homestead to their child with the understanding that the parent will continue to live there until he/she dies. But this is just trading risks.

⊠   RISK OF LOSS

Property transferred to your child could be lost if the child runs into serious financial difficulties or gets sued. This is especially a risk if your child is a professional doctor, nurse, accountant, financial planner, attorney, etc.). If your child is (or gets) married, this complicates matters even more so. If the child is divorced, the property may need to be included as part of the settlement agreement. This may be to your child's detriment because the child may need to share the value of the property with his/her former spouse. If you do not transfer the property, it cannot become part of the marital equation.

⊠ LOSS OF HOMESTEAD CREDITOR PROTECTION

Your homestead is a protected asset. With the exception of property taxes and the loan on your homestead, none of your creditors can force the sale of your property (Florida Constitution, Article X, Section 4).

If you simply transfer your homestead to a child, you lose your homestead protection against creditors. If you are married, it is a double loss of creditor protection. Not only do you lose creditor protection for yourself, you lose it for your spouse and children as well (see Chapter 5).

If your child does not occupy that property as his homestead, there is no homestead creditor protection whatsoever. The child's creditors can force the sale of the property (that's your home) for relatively small amounts of unpaid debts.

⊠ LOSS OF HOMESTEAD TAX EXEMPTION

Every homeowner whose primary residence is in the state of Florida is entitled to a Homestead Tax Exemption. Additional exemptions are allowed for any number of reasons such as the owner being a widow, or widower, or blind or permanently disabled. If you transfer your homestead, you will lose your right to receive these significant tax breaks (FS 196.031, 196.101, 196.202).

⊠ POSSIBLE GIFT TAX

If the value of the transfer is worth more than $11,000 you need to file a Gift Tax return. For most of us, this is not a problem because no Gift Tax need be paid unless the value of the property (plus the value of all gifts in excess of the Annual Gift Tax Exclusion that you gave over your lifetime) exceeds $1,000,000 (see Page 40). But if your Estate is in that tax bracket, you need to be aware that you are "using up" your lifetime Gift Tax Exclusion.

⊠ POSSIBLE CAPITAL GAINS TAX

Although Congress has expressed their intent to phase out the Estate Tax, there is no discussion to do away with the Capital Gains Tax. If you gift the property to the child during your lifetime, when he sells the property he will pay a Capital Gains Tax on the increase in value from the price you paid for your home to the selling price at the time your child sells the property.

If you do not make the gift during your lifetime, the child will inherit the property with a step-up in basis, i.e., he will inherit the property at its market value as of your date of death. Under today's tax structure and continuing until 2009, that step-up in basis is unlimited. If your child sells the property when he inherits it, he will pay no Capital Gains Tax, regardless of how large the step-up in basis.

In 2010, there will be a limit on the amount that can be inherited free of the Capital Gains Tax; but that limit is quite high, so for most of us this is not a concern.

⊠ POSSIBLE LOSS OF GOVERNMENT BENEFITS

If you transfer property, then depending upon the value of the transfer, you could be disqualified from receiving Medicaid or Supplemental Security Income ("SSI") benefits for a substantial period of time. When a person applies for Medicaid, he must disclose if, within three years of his application, he transferred property for less than the full value (i.e. he gifted property).

This reporting period extends to five years if the transfer was to a Trust. The Medicaid agency will compute a disqualification period depending on the value of the transfer. This can present a serious problem should you need extended nursing care during that period of time.

Under current state and federal law, there are many ways to protect your homestead and still qualify for government benefits. Before transferring your homestead because of your concern for the cost of future health care, consult with an Elder Law attorney. He will be able to suggest ways to protect your assets, and still ensure that you receive the health care you may require in your later years.

 **LAWYER**   OUT OF STATE PROPERTY

Each state is in charge of the way property located in that state is transferred. If you own property in another state (or country), you need to consult with an attorney in that state (or country) to determine how that property will be transferred to your beneficiaries once you die. Many state laws are similar to Florida, namely, property held as **JOINT TENANTS WITH RIGHT OF SURVIVOR** or a **LIFE ESTATE INTEREST** are transferred without the need for Probate.

If you own property in another state, in your name only, or as a **TENANT IN COMMON,** or if you hold property with your spouse in a Community Property state, a Probate procedure may need to be held in that state. If it is necessary to have a Probate proceeding in Florida, a second Probate proceeding may need to be held in the state where the property is located. This could have the effect of doubling the cost of Probate.

Still another problem is the matter of taxes. Inheritance taxes may be due in the state where the property is held. It may be necessary to file a tax return in two states. In addition to increased taxes, this can double the cost of the accounting fees.

You may wish to consult with an attorney for suggestions about how to set up your Estate Plan to avoid such problems.

A TRUST MAY BE THE SOLUTION (OR NOT)

A full Probate procedure may be necessary if you hold property in your name only or as a Tenant In Common. We explored different ways to re-title property to avoid Probate, but these methods may have trade-offs that are unacceptable to you. One way to avoid many of these potential problems is to set up a **Revocable Living Trust** (also known as an *Inter Vivos Trust*).

A Revocable Living Trust is designed to care for your property during your lifetime and then to distribute your property once you die without the need for Probate. You may have been encouraged to set up such a Trust by your financial planner, or attorney, or accountant. Even people of modest means are being encouraged to use a Trust as the basis of their Estate Plan. But Trusts have their pros and cons. Before getting into that, let's first discuss what a Trust is and how it works:

SETTING UP A TRUST

To create a Trust, an attorney prepares the Trust document in accordance with the client's needs and desires. The person who signs the document is called the *Trustor* or *Settlor.* If the *Trustor* also funds the Trust, then he is also referred to as the **Grantor.** We will refer to the Revocable Living Trust as the "Living Trust" or just the "Trust" and the person setting up the Trust as the "Grantor." The Trust document identifies who is to be the Trustee (manager) of property placed in the Trust. Usually the Grantor appoints himself as Trustee so that he is in total control of property that he places into the Trust. The Trust document also names a Successor Trustee who will take over the management of the Trust property should the Trustee resign, or become disabled or die.

Once the Trust document is properly signed, the Grantor transfers property into the Trust. The Grantor does this by changing the name on the account from his individual name to his name as Trustee. For example, if Elaine Richards sets up a Trust naming herself as Trustee, and she wishes to place her bank account into the Trust then all she need do is instruct the bank to change the name on the account from Elaine Richards to:

ELAINE RICHARDS, TRUSTEE OF THE ELAINE RICHARDS REVOCABLE TRUST AGREEMENT DATED JULY 12, 2004.

When the change is made, all the money in the account becomes Trust property. Elaine (wearing her Trustee hat) has total control of the account, taking money out, and putting money in, as she sees fit. Similarly, if she wants to put real property into the Trust all she need do is have her attorney prepare a new deed with the owner identified as ELAINE RICHARDS, TRUSTEE (see page 120 for an example of real property placed into a Trust).

The Trust document states how the Trust property is to be managed during Elaine's lifetime. Should Elaine become disabled the Trust will provide for her Successor Trustee to take over and manage the Trust funds. Because the Trust is revocable, Elaine can terminate the Trust at any time she wishes, and have all the Trust property placed back into her own individual name. If she does not revoke her Trust during her lifetime, once she dies her Successor Trustee will take over and follow the terms of the Trust Agreement as written. If the Trust says to give the Trust property to certain beneficiaries, the Successor Trustee will do so, and without the need for Probate. If the Trust directs the Successor Trustee to continue to hold property in Trust and use the money to take care of a member of Elaine's family, the Successor Trustee will do so.

Setting up a Trust has many good features.

☆☆ AVOID PROBATE

In Florida, Probate can be time consuming and very expensive. Both the Personal Representative and his attorney are entitled to payment for their services. These fees can be significant. It may be necessary to employ accountants and appraisers, and real estate brokers to sell property as well. If you have property in two states, then two Probate procedures may be necessary (one in each state) and that could have the effect of doubling the cost of Probate. If the Trust is properly drafted and your property placed into the Trust, you should be able to avoid Probate altogether.

☆ FEDERAL ESTATE TAX SAVINGS

Many people think that the federal Estate Tax will be phased out so that by 2010, no Estate Taxes will be due regardless of the size of an Estate. But under current law in 2011, the Estate Tax is scheduled to be reinstated and those who own property worth more than $1,000,000 will once again be subject to a sizeable Estate Tax. A couple with an Estate in excess of a million dollars can reduce the risk of an Estate Tax by setting up a Trust, so that each partner can take advantage of his own Estate Tax Exclusion.

For example, if a couple owns two million dollars, they can set up a Trust that separates the money into two Trusts once one partner dies. The Trust can be arranged so that the surviving spouse is free to use the income from both Trusts. Once both partners are deceased, the beneficiaries of their respective Trusts will inherit the funds, hopefully with no Estate Tax due. If the couple does not set up a Trust and continues to hold all of their property jointly, the last to die will own the two million dollars with only one Estate Tax Exclusion available.

☆ CARE FOR FAMILY MEMBER

You can make provision in your Trust to care for a minor child or family member after you die. If your family member is immature or a born spender, you can set up the Trust to protect the beneficiary from squandering his inheritance. If you are concerned that your beneficiary will spend, within months, what it took you a lifetime to earn, consider having an attorney prepare a Trust that will spread the inheritance over an extended period of time. Your Trust can direct the Successor Trustee to give a certain amount of money every five or ten years; for example you can direct the Trustee to give part of the gift when the beneficiary reaches 25, another amount when he reaches 35, and then 45, etc.

If your intended beneficiary has a creditor problem, you can set up a *Spendthrift Trust*. You can direct your Successor Trustee to use the Trust funds for your beneficiary's health care, education, and living expenses, and nothing else. With a properly drafted Spendthrift Trust provision the Trust funds should be protected from the claims of the creditors of the beneficiary.

NO CREDITOR PROTECTION FOR GRANTOR

Although you can set up a Spendthrift Trust for the benefit of a family member, you cannot set one up for yourself. Property you place in your Revocable Living Trust is freely accessible to you. It is likewise accessible to your creditors both before and after your death. Under Florida law, upon your death, the Successor Trustee must file a Notice of Trust with the Probate Court. If you die owing money, your creditors can have a Personal Representative appointed to locate funds to pay those debts. The Personal Representative can require that your Trust property be used to pay for those debts as well as for other expenses associated with the Probate procedure (FS 737.3054, 737.308).

☆ PRIVACY

Your Living Trust is a private document. No one but your Successor Trustee and your beneficiaries need ever read it. If you leave property in a Will and there is a Probate procedure, the Will must be filed with the Court, where it becomes a public document. Anyone can go to the courthouse, read your Will and see who you did (or did not) provide for in your Will. Records in the Probate Court (inventories, creditor's claims, etc.) are open to public scrutiny. In fact, many counties within the state of Florida now publish certain Court records on the Internet!

LEASE SAFE DEPOSIT BOX AS TRUSTEE

One of the benefits of having a Living Trust is that you can lease the safe deposit box in your name as Trustee. When you lease the safe deposit box you can have an agreement with the bank that they are to allow your Successor Trustee free access to the safe deposit box in the event of your incapacity or death.

This protects your privacy. As explained in Chapter 3, if you hold the safe deposit box in your name only, access to the box is restricted upon your death. No one can take possession of the contents of your box without a Court order, but your next of kin can ask the bank to be allowed to examine the contents of the box to see if your Will is there. Under Florida law the bank can allow such inspection, provided a bank officer or employee is present when the contents of the box are examined (FS 655.935).

By leasing a safe deposit box as Trustee, only you and your Successor Trustee need ever know of the contents of the box.

☆☆ AVOID APPOINTMENT OF A GUARDIAN

Once you have a Trust you do not need to worry about who will take care of your property should you become disabled or too aged to handle your finances. The person you appoint as Successor Trustee will take over the care of the Trust property if you are unable to do so. If you do not make provision for the care of your property, it may be necessary for a Court to appoint a Guardian of your property. Guardianship is a good thing to avoid, not only because of the cost of the procedure, but also to avoid the embarrassment of a Court coming to the conclusion that you are not competent to manage your own finances.

Before appointing a Guardian, the Court will have a hearing to determine whether you competent to manage your property. You are entitled to your own attorney at the hearing. If you do not have one the Court will appoint an attorney for you. If the judge decides that you do not have the capacity to handle your finances, he will appoint a Guardian. He may order the Guardian to obtain a bond for the protection of your property. Once appointed, the Guardian will take possession of your property and file an inventory with the Court. The Guardian will manage your property and each year account to the Court for monies spent He may need to employ an accountant to assist with these reports. The Guardian needs to employ an attorney to establish the Guardianship and see to it that it is properly administered. The Guardian and his attorney are entitle to be paid for their efforts on your behalf (FS 744.331, 744.351, 744.361).

Court filing fees, the cost of a bond, accounting fees, Guardian's fees, attorney's fees for you and the Guardian, are all paid from your Estate (that's your money!). And this expense goes on year after year until you are restored to capacity or die.

THE PROBLEMS

⊠ COMPLEXITY

A Trust is a fairly complex document, often more than 20 pages long. It needs to be that long because you are establishing a vehicle to care for your property during your lifetime, as well as after your death. Your Trust may be written in "legalese," so it may take you considerable time and effort to understand it. It is important to have your Trust document prepared by an attorney who has the patience to work with you until you fully understand each paragraph of the document and are satisfied that what it states is what you really want.

It is also important that you read Florida statute 737.402. That statute gives your Successor Trustee the power to do all of the things as allowed by that statute, unless your Trust specifically prohibits your Successor Trustee from doing so. For example, under 737.402, your Trustee has the power to terminate the Trust whenever the market value of the Trust property is $50,000 or less. If you have included a Spendthrift Trust, you may not want your Successor Trustee to just hand $50,000 to your beneficiary. In such case, it is important that your Trust Agreement state that 737.402 shall not apply to the termination of the Spendthrift Trust.

⊠ COST

Because of the thoroughness of the document and the fact that it is custom designed for you, a Trust will cost much more to draft than a simple Will. In addition to the initial cost of the Trust, it can be expensive to maintain the Trust should you become disabled or die. Your Successor Trustee has the right to charge for his duties as Trustee, as well as to charge for any specialized services performed.

A financial institution can charge to serve as Successor Trustee, and also charge to manage the Trust portfolio. If you decide to have a financial institution serve as Trustee, then it is important that you compare the fee schedules of different institutions.

If you choose a professional (lawyer, accountant, financial planner, etc.) to serve as Trustee, it is important to have a fee agreement stating what will be charged for his duties as Trustee and what will be charged for professional work done on behalf of the Trust. If you make no provision, the professional is entitled to the going rate for work done in relation to a Trust. And that fee can be substantial. Under Florida law, a reasonable fee for a Trustee's attorney is 75% of the schedule charged by the attorney of a Probate Estate (see page 160) (FS 737.2041).

Still another concern with choosing a professional to serve as Trustee is that it creates a conflict of interest. The professional can use his position as Trustee to generate fees for himself or his firm.

You may decide to appoint your spouse or a family member as Successor Trustee, who may want little, or no, compensation. Regardless of who you choose to be Successor Trustee, you need to come to an agreement as to what will be charged to manage the Trust. If you make no provision for fees in your Trust Agreement, your Successor Trustee has the right to take a reasonable fee from the Trust property. If the beneficiaries of the Trust do not think the fee reasonable, they can ask to the Court to set the fee (FS 737.204).

But that will probably trigger a legal battle. It is better that you set the fee. Hopefully, that will head off unnecessary legal fees.

⊠ YOU MAY NEED YOUR SPOUSE'S PERMISSION TO TRANSFER PROPERTY INTO YOUR TRUST

Most married couples prepare a Trust as part of their overall Estate Plan. Sometimes a married person has a Trust that was prepared prior to the marriage, or he may decide to create a Trust to care for children from a previous marriage. In such case, it may be necessary to have the spouse agree, in writing, to transfers into the Trust. The reason permission is needed is the *Elective Share*. The Grantor's spouse has a right to inherit at least as much as allowed under Florida law, unless the spouse signs a waiver giving up that right. In Florida, the Elective Share is equal to 30% of the *Elective Estate* of the decedent spouse (FS 732.201, 732.2065).

The Elective Estate includes:

⇨ Property held in the decedent's Living Trust

⇨ The decedent's Probate Estate

⇨ The decedent's ownership interest in joint bank accounts, In Trust For or Pay On Death accounts, Transfer On Death securities, etc.

⇨ Transfers made within the year prior to death that the Court determines were made to avoid the Elective Share. The proceeds of a life insurance policy are not included in the Elective Estate, however, the cash surrender value of the policy immediately before the date of death is included (FS 732.2045). See FS 732.2035 for a complete list of property included in the Elective Estate.

If you make transfers into your Trust without your spouse's permission, and without providing that your spouse receive 30% of your Elective Estate, your spouse can go to the Probate Court and demand that as much property be transferred from the Trust (or from anyone in possession of your property) as is necessary to make up the Elective Share (FS 732.2145).

⊠ PROBATE MIGHT STILL BE NECESSARY

The Trust only works for those items that you place in the Trust. If you own property in your name only, then upon your death, a Probate procedure might be necessary in order to transfer the property to your beneficiary. For example, if you purchase a security in your name only, without a "Transfer On Death" designation to a named beneficiary or to your Trust, then a Probate procedure may be necessary to determine who should inherit the security.

The attorney who prepares the Trust usually creates a safety net for such situations. He prepares a Will for you to sign at the same time you sign the Trust. The Will makes your Trust the beneficiary of your Probate Estate. If you own anything in your name only and a Probate procedure is necessary, the Will directs your Personal Representative to make that asset part of your Trust by transferring the asset to your Successor Trustee. Your Successor Trustee will add that asset to your Trust.

The Will prepared by the attorney is called a "Pour Over Will" because it is designed to "pour" any asset titled in your name only, into the Trust. Having the Will ensures that all of your property will go to the beneficiaries named in your Trust. But the downside of holding property in your name only is that a full Probate procedure may be necessary just to get that asset into your Trust. If avoiding Probate is your goal, holding property, in your name only, defeats that goal.

You can ensure that a Probate procedure will not be necessary by transferring your assets into your Trust during your lifetime, but if you neglect to put something into your Trust, the Pour Over Will stands by to transfer that asset into your Trust.

⊠ TAXES MAY STILL BE A PROBLEM

While you are operating the Trust as Trustee, all of the property held in your Revocable Living Trust is taxed as if you were holding that property in your own name. If the value of your Trust property exceeds the Estate and/or Gift Tax Exclusion value, taxes will be due and owing once you die. For those in that fortunate tax bracket, an experienced financial planner or tax attorney can suggest other, more advanced, Estate Planning strategies to reduce taxes.

⊠ ☆ THE TRUST IS LEGALLY ENFORCEABLE

Your Successor Trustee will take over the administration of your death upon your incapacity or death. Should there be a dispute regarding the administration of the Trust, your beneficiary, or the Successor Trustee, can petition the Court to settle the matter. For example, if the Trustee is abusing his power or not accounting for Trust funds, the beneficiaries can ask the Court to have the Trustee removed (FS 737.201, 737.303).

We gave this section a cross and a star, because the right to have a Trust enforced or administered by the Court is a double edged sword. It is great to have the Court protect the rights of your beneficiaries, but the cost of a court battle could be greater than if your Estate was subject to Probate in the first place. Your beneficiaries are at a financial disadvantage. The Court can require your Trustee to be personally liable for legal costs, but that only happens if the Trustee acted illegally or unreasonably. In most cases, the Trustee will be able to charge attorney fees to defend his actions to the Trust (FS 737.2035). Your beneficiaries will pay for their legal expenses out of their own pockets. Win or lose, there will be just that much less for your beneficiaries to inherit.

⊠ BENEFICIARIES CAN CHANGE THE TRUST

The Florida legislature passed a law (FS 737.4032) that effectively gives the Successor Trustee and the beneficiaries of the Trust, the power to do whatever they wish with Trust property once the Grantor dies. Specifically, for Trusts created after January 1, 2001, regardless of what the Trust says, and regardless of the fact that upon the death of the Grantor, the Trust becomes irrevocable, the Trustee, with the unanimous agreement of all of the beneficiaries, can do any of the following:

⇨ Change any of the terms on the Trust, including changing the beneficiaries of the Trust and/or the income or principal each beneficiary is to receive.

⇨ Terminate the Trust altogether

⇨ Stop the Successor Trustee from doing things required by the Trust Agreement

⇨ Allow the Successor Trustee to do things strictly prohibited by the Trust Agreement.

Used to be once the Grantor died the Trust could be changed only if there was good reason to do so, and only if a Court gave permission for the change. With this new law, the Successor Trustee and beneficiaries can agree do whatever they wish, regardless of what the Trust says, and without asking Court permission to do so.

If this new law is of concern to you, consult with an experienced Estate Planning attorney. He will be able to suggest any number of ways to avoid having your Successor Trustee and beneficiaries change your Estate plan.

MAYBE PROBATE ISN'T ALL THAT BAD

Although all of the methods discussed in this Chapter can be used to transfer property without the need for Probate, it may be each method has a downside that is objectionable to you. Maybe you don't have enough money to warrant the cost of setting up the Trust at this time. Holding property jointly with another may raise issues of security and independence. Holding property so that it goes directly to a few beneficiaries in a Pay-On-Death account, may not be as flexible as you wish.

This is especially the case if you wish to give gifts to several charities or to minor children instead of just one or two beneficiaries. For example, if you hold all your property so that it goes to your son without the need for Probate, and you ask him to use some of the money for your grandchild's education, it may be that your grandchild gets none of the money because your son is sued or falls upon hard times. If you keep your property in your name only and leave a Will giving a certain amount of money for your grandchild, the child will know exactly how much money you left and the purpose of that gift.

After taking into account all the pros and cons of avoiding Probate, you may well opt for a Will and a Probate procedure. If you make such a decision, it is important to keep in mind that Estate Planning is not an "all or nothing" choice. You can arrange your Estate so that certain items pass automatically to your intended beneficiary, and other items can be left in your name only, to be distributed as part of a Probate procedure. By arranging your finances in this manner, you can reduce the value of your Probate Estate, and that in turn should reduce the cost of Probate.

Your Florida Will 8

Many people decide that the Will is the best route to go but do not act upon it, thinking it unnecessary to prepare a Will until they are very old and about to die. But according to reports published by the National Center for Health Statistics (a division of the U.S. Department of Health and Human Services) 2 of every 10 people who die in any given year are under the age of 60.

Twenty percent may seem like a small number until it hits close to home as it did with a young couple. They were having difficulty conceiving a child. They went from doctor to doctor until they met someone just beginning his practice. With his knowledge of the latest advances in medicine, he was able to help them.

The birth of their child was a moment of joy and gratitude. They asked a nurse to take a picture of them all together — the proud parents, the newborn child and the doctor who made it all possible. Happiness radiated from the picture, but within 6 months, one of them would be dead.

You might think it was the child. An infant's life is so fragile. SIDS and all manner of childhood diseases can threaten a little one. But no, he grew up a healthy young man.

If you looked at the picture, you might guess the husband. Overweight and stressed out; his ruddy complexion suggested high blood pressure. He looked like a typical heart- attack-prone type A personality.

No, he was fine and went on to enjoy raising his son.

Probably the wife. She had such a difficult time with the pregnancy and the delivery was especially hard. Perhaps it was all too much for her. No, she recovered and later had two more children.

It was the doctor who was killed in a collision with a truck.

WHY A WILL IS NECESSARY

Though we all agree, that one never knows, still people put off making a Will figuring that if they die before getting around to it, Florida law will take over and their property will be distributed in the manner that they would have wanted anyway. The problem with that logic is the complexity of Florida's Laws of Intestate Succession. If you are survived by a spouse, child, parent or sibling, then it isn't too difficult to figure out who will inherit your property. But if none of these survive you, the ultimate beneficiary of your property may not be the person you would have chosen, had you taken the time to do so.

Others think that it is not necessary to have a Will because they have arranged their finances so that all of their property will be inherited without the need for Probate. But money could come into your Estate after your death. This could happen in any number of ways from winning the lottery and dying (of happiness, no doubt) to receiving insurance funds after your death. For example, if you die in a house fire or flood the insurance company may need to pay for damage done to your property. In such case, a Personal Representative may need to be appointed and the monies distributed according to Florida law.

If you die without a Will, the Personal Representative may not be the person you would have chosen. The monies may be distributed differently than you would have wished. And as explained in this Chapter, there are other important reasons to make a Will.

SET THE PERSONAL REPRESENTATIVE'S FEE

An important reason to make a Will is so that you can choose your Personal Representative and come to an understanding about how much compensation he is to receive. You can state that value in your Will.

CAUTION THE PERSONAL REPRESENTATIVE CAN SEEK MORE MONEY

Even though your Will states the amount of compensation to be given to your Personal Representative, he may decide the job was more work than he expected. He may ask the Probate Court to award the amount determined as "reasonable" by Florida statute. To avoid the problem, you can have you attorney draft a Fee Agreement that you both sign and attach to your Will.

Having a separate fee Agreement will not stop your Personal Representative from asking for more money, but with such an Agreement, the Court will not agree to the increase unless something unusual occurs (such as a law suit) causing much more work than the ordinary Probate proceeding.

You also need to keep in mind that the Personal Representative's fee is just to administer the Estate. It does not include payment for professional work he may do while settling the Estate. For example, if you appoint your attorney as Personal Representative, he can agree to the amount stated in the Will for his role as Personal Representative, and then ask the Court to award him attorney's fees as well. And those fees are substantial (see Page 159).

The same goes for any other professional. If you appoint your accountant to serve as Personal Representative, he is entitled to receive compensation for his work as Personal Representative and also for any accounting work he does such as preparing and filing tax returns; preparing an inventory and doing an accounting for the beneficiaries. A financial planner who serves as Personal Representative may be compensated for his management of the Estate property (buying and selling securities, taking care of rental property, etc.) in addition to his fee to administer the Estate.

But the main problem with appointing a professional as your Personal Representative is the same as appointing a professional to serve as the Successor Trustee of your Trust; namely, that it creates a potential conflict of interest. The professional can use his position as Personal Representative to generate fees that may not have been necessary if someone else settled the Estate. Unless the professional is the sole beneficiary of your Estate, consider choosing a non-professional for the job.

MAKE GIFTS OF YOUR PERSONAL PROPERTY

Another benefit to making a Will is that you can make gifts of your personal property, including your car. If you make a gift of your car in your Will, it will be relatively simple for your car to be transferred to that beneficiary. If you do not make a specific gift of your car, it becomes part of your Probate Estate. Your Personal Representative will decide what to do with it. He can sell it and include the proceeds of the sale in the Estate funds to be distributed to your residuary beneficiaries; or he can give the car to one beneficiary of your Estate as part of that beneficiary's share of the Estate.

SMALL GIFTS MATTER

Many who have lost someone close to them report that the distribution of small personal items caused the greatest conflict. If you arrange your finances so that no Probate proceeding is necessary, your next of kin will need to decide how to distribute your personal effects. Without guidance from you and no Representative with authority to make decisions, there could be much disagreement and hard feelings, over items of little monetary value.

Under Florida law, you can make gifts of your personal effects (record collection, books, jewelry etc.) by making a list of these gifts and attaching it to your Will. Your Personal Representative will distribute your personal effects according to that list. You can change the list at any time just so long as you sign and date the list. No witness to your signature is needed. The list is for items with more sentimental than monetary value. You should not include money gifts, securities or real property in the list. Those items need to be given as part of your Will (FS 732.515).

Of course, you cannot make a list of each and every item you own, but you can instruct your Personal Representative to allow certain family members to take their choice of items not mentioned in your Will. If two or more family members want the same item, have your Personal Representative use an appropriate lottery system (coin toss, high card in a cut of a deck of cards, etc.) to decide who "wins."

MAKE ADJUSTMENT FOR PRIOR GIFTS

You can use your Will to make adjustments for gifts or loans given during your lifetime. For example, if you loaned money to a family member and do not expect to be repaid, you can deduct the loan from that person's inheritance. Of course, it may be that you are not concerned with inequities. That was the case of an aged woman who had three children, Paul, Rita and Frank, her youngest. Frank always seemed to need some assistance from his mother. She often "loaned" him money he never repaid.

Her other children were responsible and independent. Paul was married and had children of his own. He decided to purchase a house but was having trouble accumulating the down payment. His mother agreed to lend him the money. Paul and his wife offered to give his mother a mortgage on the property. The mother said a simple promissory note from Paul was sufficient, and she would have her attorney draft the note.

The attorney drafted the note but was concerned about the inequity "You never made a Will. Were you to die, each of your children will inherit an equal amount of money. If Paul still owes money on this promissory note, he will either need to pay the balance to your Estate, or have it subtracted from the amount he inherits. All of the money you gave to Frank will not count towards his inheritance unless you make your intentions clear that you considered the money you gave to Frank to be an advancement of his inheritance. You can do this by making an adjustment in a Will, or by having Frank give you a promissory note for any outstanding debts.

"It's O.K." replied the mother "I love all my children equally . . . some are a little more equal than others."

Property held in a Pay On Death account, the proceeds of a life insurance policy, Trust property and IRA accounts are all *Non-probate* assets because they will be inherited by your named beneficiary without the need for Probate. You cannot make a gift of such property in your Will because, you have, in effect, already made a gift of these assets. The beneficiary of a Non-probate asset can only be changed by the owner of the property during his lifetime. The beneficiary of a Non-probate asset cannot be changed by Will (FS 711.509). Unless you named your Estate as the beneficiary of a Non-probate asset, it should not be mentioned in your Will. To do so might cause your Will to be challenged by whoever was named as the beneficiary of the Non-probate asset.

THE SPOUSE'S RIGHT TO A LIFE ESTATE

If your Florida home is in your name only, and it is your primary residence, then under Florida law, your surviving spouse has the right to continue to live in your home for the rest of his/her life. Once your spouse is deceased, your children inherit the home in equal shares, per stirpes. You can make a Will giving the house to your spouse, but only if you do not have minor children. If you have minor children, regardless of what your Will says, your spouse has a Life Estate with remainder to your children (FS 732.401, 732.4015).

If you want your spouse to inherit your home, minor children or not, have your attorney change the deed so that your home is owned by you and your spouse as Tenants by the Entirety.

MINOR CHILD'S RIGHT TO THE HOMESTEAD

Married or single, if you have minor children, they have rights in your homestead. Specifically, under the Florida Constitution, if you own your home in your name only and are single with minor children, with or without a Will your children inherit your homestead, in equal shares, per stirpes (Florida Constitution Article X, Section 4(c)).

Of course, if you are single, without minor children, you are free to give that property to any beneficiary you name in your Will.

📄 CHOOSE A GUARDIAN FOR YOUR MINOR CHILD

If a parent dies, it is the right, and duty, of the surviving parent to care for the child (FS 744.301). But it could happen that both parents become incapacitated or die before the child is grown. If you have a minor child, you can use your Will to appoint someone to serve as the Guardian of your minor child in the event that both you and the other parent are deceased (FS 744.312). You can even include a Trust in your Will, naming someone to serve as Trustee to care for property that you leave to your minor child.

Some people think that preparing a Will is a simple thing — something they can do themselves. But writing a Will is like figure skating. It is harder than it looks. A Will needs to be clearly worded. A sentence that can be read in two different ways can lead to a dispute over what you intended; and that could result in a long and expensive Court battle. The Will must be signed and witnessed according to Florida law, otherwise the Judge may refuse to admit the Will to Probate, and your property will be distributed as if you had no Will at all.

As explained in Chapter 5, there are any number of reasons to challenge a Will. If you want to be assured that your Will is honored, it is best to have an Estate Planning attorney, prepare a Will according to your directions and then supervise the signing of your Will.

STORING THE WILL

Once you sign your Will, you may wonder where to store it. Your attorney may suggest that he place it in his vault for safekeeping. By doing so, he ensures that your heirs will contact him as soon as you die. This does not mean that they are required to employ him should a Probate proceeding be necessary. It only means that he will have an opportunity for future employment.

But there are problems with such an arrangement. The Will could be lost or mistaken for another Will. That happened in at least one case. The attorney prepared Wills for two people with the same name and similar family circumstances. When one person died the attorney submitted the wrong Will to Probate.

If you decided to allow your attorney to store the Will, you need assurances that the attorney will be responsible for the document. You should get a receipt and something in writing that says:

⇨ The attorney accepts full responsibility for the storage of the Will. Should it be lost or damaged, he will replace the document at no cost to you; and if you are deceased, he will, at no cost to your heirs, present sufficient evidence to the Court to accept a valid copy of the Will into Probate.

⇨ There will be no charge to you, or your heirs, for the storage and retrieval of the document.

⇨ Should he sell his practice, retire, or die, he or the successor to his practice, will return the original document to you.

THE SAFE DEPOSIT BOX, SAFE BUT . . .

You might consider placing your document in a safe deposit box that you lease at a bank. The only problem with the bank safe deposit box is convenient access. If you hold a safe deposit box in your name only, should you die, the bank will restrict access to the safe deposit box. Under Florida law, your spouse, child, parent, or person named as Personal Representative of your Will can inspect the contents of your safe box provided they do so under the supervision of a bank employee (FS 655.935). If your Will is there, the bank can forward it to the Probate Court.

Other than your Will, deed to burial plot, and insurance policy, nothing can be removed without authority from the Probate Court.

Once a Personal Representative is appointed by the Court, he will have such authority. He will be able to take possession of the contents of your safe deposit box. But if you arranged your finances to avoid Probate, it is self defeating to trigger a Probate procedure just to get the contents of the box (FS 655.936, 733.6065).

For those who are married, the solution to the problem of accessing the safe deposit box after death, is to lease the box jointly with your spouse, such that each of you has free access to the box. Those who have a Trust can solve the problem by giving their Successor Trustee joint access to the safe deposit box. If you are single and do not have a Trust, you can lease the box jointly with a trusted family member. Of course, if privacy and security are important to you, then that may outweigh any concern for the convenience of your beneficiaries.

Regardless of where you choose to store your Will, let your Personal Representative know that you have a Will and how to retrieve it in the event of your death.

CHOOSING THE RIGHT ESTATE PLAN

Joint Ownership?
A POD Account?
A TOD Security?
A Trust?
A Will?
An Insurance Policy???

Chapters 7 and 8 offer so many options that the reader may be more confused than when he was blissfully unenlightened.

As with most things in life, you may find there are no ultimate solutions, just alternatives. The right choice for you is the one that best accomplishes your goal. This being the case, you first need to determine what you want to accomplish with the money you leave. Think about what will happen to your property if you were to die suddenly, without making any plan different from the one you now have.

>   Who will be responsible to pay your bills?
>   Who will get your property?
>   Will Probate be necessary?

If the answers to these questions are not what you wish, then you need to work to arrange your property to accomplish your goals.

For those with significant assets, — especially those with Estates large enough to pay Estate taxes, a trip to an experienced Estate Planning attorney may be well worth the consultation fee.

Your Estate Plan Record 9

Once you are satisfied with your Estate Plan, then the final thing to consider is whether your heirs will be able to locate your assets once you are gone.

Most people have their business records in one place, their Will in another place, car titles and deeds in still another place. When someone dies, their beneficiaries may feel as if they are playing a game of "hide and seek" with the decedent. The game might be fun were it not for the fact that an unlocated item may be forever lost. For example, suppose you die in an accident and no one knows you are insured by your credit card company for accidental death in the amount of $25,000. The only one to profit is the insurance company, which is just that much richer because no one told them that you died as a result of an accident.

And how about a key to a safe deposit box located in another state? Will anyone find it? Even if they find the key, how will they find the box?

It is not difficult to arrange things so that your affairs are always in order. It amounts to being aware of what you own (and owe) and keeping a record of your possessions. A side benefit is that by doing so, you will always know where all your business records are. If you ever spent time trying to collect information to file your taxes or trying to find a lost stock or bond certificate, you will appreciate the value of organizing your records.

ORGANIZING YOUR RECORDS

Heirs need all the help they can get. It is difficult enough dealing with the loss, without the frustration of trying to locate important documents. Your heirs will have no problem locating your assets if you keep all of your records in a single place. It can be a desk drawer or a file cabinet or even a shoe box. It is helpful if you keep a separate file or folder for each type of investment. You might consider setting up the following folders:

🗁 THE BANK & SECURITIES FOLDER

Store your original certificates for stocks, bonds, mutual funds, certificates of deposit, in a folder labeled **BANK & SECURITIES FOLDER**. In addition to the original certificate include a copy of the contract you signed with each financial institution. The contract will show where you have funds and who you named as beneficiary or joint owner of the account. If someone owes you money and signed a promissory note or mortgage identifying you as the lender, store these documents in this folder as well.

If you have a safe deposit box, keep a record of its location and the number of the box. Keep a copy of all of the items stored in the box in this folder. If you have an extra key to the box, put it here.

E-bank Accounts If you are doing your banking on-line, it is important to keep a record of your passwords so that your family can access the account in the event of your incapacity or death. The same applies if you have on-line brokerage or installment loan accounts. Keep a paper record of these account in this folder.

🗂 THE INSURANCE FOLDER

The INSURANCE FOLDER is for each insurance policy that you own, be it life insurance, car insurance, homeowner's insurance or a health care insurance policy. If you purchased real property, you probably received a title commitment at closing and the title insurance policy some weeks later when you received your original deed from recording. If you cannot locate the title insurance policy, contact the closing agent and have him send you a copy of your title policy.

🗂 THE PENSION AND ANNUITY FOLDER

If you have a Pension or Annuity, put all of the documents relating to the Pension in this folder. Include the telephone number and/or address of the person to contact in the event of your death.

FOR FEDERAL RETIREES If you are a Federal Retiree, you should have received your PERSONAL IDENTIFICATION NUMBER (PIN) and the person who will inherit your pension (your *survivor annuitant*) should have his/her own PIN as well. It is relatively simple to obtain this during your lifetime, but it may be difficult and/or stressful for your survivor annuitant to work through the system once you are gone.

Survivor annuitant benefits are not automatic. Your survivor annuitant must apply for them by submitting a death claim to the Office of Personnel Management. Your survivor needs to know that it is necessary to apply and also how to apply. You can get printed information about how to apply from the Office Of Personnel Management (see Page 34). Keep the printed information in this file.

🗁 THE DEED FOLDER

Many people save every scrap of paper associated with the closing of real property. If you closed recently on real estate and there was a mortgage involved in the purchase, you probably walked away from closing with enough paper to wallpaper your kitchen. If you wish, you can keep all of those papers in a separate file that identifies the property, for example:

CLOSING PAPERS FOR THE MIAMI PROPERTY

Place the original deed (or a copy if the original is in a safe deposit box) in a separate **DEED FOLDER**. Include cemetery deeds, condominium deeds, cooperative shares to real property, timesharing certificates, deed to out of state property, etc. Also include a copy of related documents such as an Abstract of Title, or a recorded Condominium Approval. If you have a title insurance policy, put the original in the insurance folder, and a copy in this folder. If you have a mortgage on your property, put a copy of the recorded mortgage and promissory note in a separate **LIABILITY FOLDER**.

LOCATING REAL PROPERTY

If you own a vacant lot, your beneficiaries will find the deed (or a copy) in this folder but that deed will not contain the address of that property because it doesn't have one. The post office does not assign a street address until there is a building on the site. Your beneficiaries can get the location of the property from city or county records. But why make things hard for them? Include a handwritten note in this folder that tells them exactly how to locate the property.

📁 THE LIABILITY FOLDER

The LIABILITY FOLDER should contain all loan documents of debts that you owe. For example, if you purchased real property and have a mortgage on that property, put a copy of the mortgage and promissory note in this folder. If you owe money on a car, put the loan documents in this folder. If you have a credit card, put a copy of the contract you signed with the credit card company in this folder. A lease is a liability, because you have contracted to pay a certain amount for the period of the lease, so include a copy of any lease agreement in this folder.

Many people never take the time to calculate their net worth (what a person owns less what that person owes). By having a record of your assets and outstanding debts, you can calculate your net worth whenever you wish.

📁 THE ESTATE PLANNING DOCUMENT FOLDER

Place your Estate Planning documents (Will, Trust, Pre-nuptial Agreement, burial, funeral arrangements, etc.) in a separate folder. If your attorney has your original documents, or you put the original in a safe deposit box, place a copy of the document in this folder together with instructions about how to find the original. It is important to keep a copy of your Will or Trust because over the years you may forget what provision you made. Keeping a copy in your home may save you a trip to the safe deposit box to determine whether you need to update the document.

THE PERSONAL PROPERTY FOLDER

MOTOR VEHICLES

Put all motor vehicle titles in a Personal Property folder. This includes cars, mobile homes, boats, planes, etc. If you owe money on the vehicle, the lender may have possession of the title certificate. If such is the case, put a copy of the title certificate and registration in this folder and a copy of the loan documents in a separate liability folder.

If you own a boat or plane, identify the location of the motor vehicle. For example, if you are leasing space in an airplane hangar or in a marina, keep a copy of the leasing agreement in this file.

JEWELRY

If you own expensive jewelry, keep a picture of the item together with the sales receipt or written appraisal in this folder.

COLLECTOR'S ITEMS

If you own a valuable art or coin collection, or any other item of significant value, include a picture of the item in this file. Also include evidence of ownership of the item, such as a sales receipt or a certificate of authenticity, or a written appraisal of the property.

📁 THE PERSONAL RECORDS FOLDER

The PERSONAL RECORDS FOLDER should include documents that relate to you personally, such as a birth certificate, naturalization papers, pre-nuptial or post-nuptial agreement, marriage certificate, divorce papers, military records, social security card; etc. If you have a Power of Attorney or a Health Care Directive, you can place the document in this folder, or in your Estate Planning folder. If you placed the original document in a safe deposit box, keep a copy in this folder together with the location of the original.

📁 THE TAX RECORD FOLDER

Your Personal Representative (or next of kin) will need to file your final income tax returns. Keep a copy of your tax returns (both federal and state) for the past three years in your Tax Record Folder.

As explained in Chapter 2, beginning in 2010, there will be a cap on the step-up basis to 4.3 million dollars for property inherited by the spouse and 1.3 million dollars for property inherited by anyone else. It is important to keep a record of the basis of your property, not only for your heirs, but for yourself should you decide to sell the property during your lifetime. If you purchase real property, you need to keep a record of the purchase price as well as monies you paid to improve the property. You will need these records to determine whether there will be a Capital Gains Tax on the transfer. Your accountant can help you set up a bookkeeping system to keep a running record of your basis in everything you own of value.

THE *If I Die* FILE

Many do not have the time, nor inclination, to "play" with all these folders. They do not anticipate an immediate demise. Getting hit by a truck, or dying in a fiery plane crash is not something to think about, much less prepare for. But consider that death is not the only problem. You could take suddenly ill (say with a stroke) and become incapacitated. Even the most time-starved optimist should have a murmur of concern that his loved ones will be left with a mess should something unforeseen happen.

If you do not feel like doing a complete job of organizing your records at this time, consider an abridged version. You can set up a single file with a list of all you own and the location of each item. You need to make that file easily accessible to whomever you wish to manage your affairs in the event of your incapacity or death. You can do this by letting that person know of the existence of the file and how to get it in an emergency; or keep the file in an easily accessible place in your home with the succinct but attention-grabbing title of *"If I Die."*

We have included a form on the next page that you can use as a basis for information to be included in the file.

If I Die

the following information will help settle my Estate:

INFORMATION FOR DEATH CERTIFICATE

MY FULL LEGAL NAME _____

MY SOCIAL SECURITY NO. _____

MY USUAL OCCUPATION _____

BIRTH DATE AND BIRTH PLACE _____

If naturalized, date & place _____

MY FATHER'S NAME _____

MY MOTHER'S MAIDEN NAME _____

PEOPLE TO BE NOTIFIED

_____

_____

_____

FUNERAL AND BURIAL ARRANGEMENTS

LOCATION OF BURIAL SITE

_____

LOCATION OF PREPAID FUNERAL CONTRACT

_____

FOR VETERAN or SPOUSE BURIAL IN A NATIONAL CEMETERY

BRANCH_____SERIAL NO._____

VETERAN'S RANK _____

VETERAN'S VA CLAIM NUMBER _____

DATE AND PLACE OF ENTRY INTO SERVICE:

_____

DATE AND PLACE OF SEPARATION FROM SERVICE:

_____

LOCATION OF OFFICIAL MILITARY DISCHARGE

OR DD 214 FORM_____

LOCATION OF LEGAL DOCUMENTS

BIRTH CERTIFICATE _____

MARRIAGE CERTIFICATE _____

DIVORCE DECREE _____

PASSPORT _____

WILL OR TRUST _____

DEEDS _____

MORTGAGES _____

TITLE TO MOTOR VEHICLES _____

HEALTH CARE DIRECTIVES _____

Name, telephone of attorney _____

LOCATION OF FINANCIAL RECORDS

INSURANCE POLICIES:
Name of Company, Location of Policy, Insurance Agent

_____

_____

PENSIONS/ANNUITIES:
IF FEDERAL RETIREE: PIN NUMBER: _____

NAME OF SURVIVOR _____

SURVIVOR PIN NUMBER _____

BANK
Name and address of Bank, Account Number,
Location of Safe Deposit Box and Key

_____

_____

SECURITIES
Name and telephone number of broker

_____

TAX RECORDS FOR PAST 3 YEARS
LOCATION _____

Name and telephone number of accountant

_____

KEEPING UP TO DATE

We discussed people's natural disinclination to make an Estate Plan until they are faced with their own mortality. Many believe that they will make just one Will and then die (maybe that's why they put off making a Will). The reality is, most people who make a Will change it at least once before they die. If you have an Estate Plan, it is important to update it when any of the following events take place:

✍ A CHANGE IN RELATIONSHIP

If you marry, divorce, have a child, or if a beneficiary of your Estate dies, you need to examine your Estate Plan to determine whether it needs to be revised. If you decide that your Will needs a complete revision, then it is important to have a new Will prepared. If you simply rip up the old Will, that will effectively revoke the Will (FS 732.506). But it could happen that someone (perhaps your attorney) has a copy of the Will. If no one knows that you revoked the Will, they may think the Will is lost and offer the copy of the Will for Probate (see page 83). If you draft a new Will, the first paragraph should say, "I revoke all prior Wills ..."

BENEFICIARY MOVES OR DIES

Most people remember to name an alternate beneficiary should one of their beneficiaries die. But how many of us remember to notify the pension plan or insurance company when a beneficiary moves? Many life insurance proceeds are never paid because the company cannot locate the beneficiary. The Actuarial Office of the Federal Employees' Group Life Insurance Program reported that as of September, 2003, they had over 55.8 million dollars in unpaid benefits, mostly because they could not locate the beneficiary at the last given address.

✍ CHANGE IN MARITAL STATUS

The minute you say "I do," your spouse has the right to occupy the property that you own as your primary residence in the state of Florida. Your spouse has this Life Estate interest regardless of whether you bought the property with just your own money; regardless of how long you owned the property; regardless of the fact that only your name appears on the deed to the property (see page 129). Once you marry, you cannot make any transfer of your Florida homestead property unless your spouse, signs a waiver of these rights, or agrees to the change and signs the deed of transfer.

Under Florida law, should you divorce and then die before you get around to changing your Will, any gift that you made in your Will or Trust for your former spouse is revoked. Your Probate Estate will be distributed as if your spouse died before you did. A legal separation in the state of Florida does not end the marriage, so these laws do not apply to couples who are separated, legally, or otherwise (FS 732.507, 737.106).

If you divorce (or even separate) it is important to review all of your Estate Planning documents (deeds, pension plans, insurance policies, Will or Trust etc.) to determine whether you wish to name a new beneficiary of your property.

NOTIFY EMPLOYER OF CHANGE

If you change your marital status (either marry or divorce) you need to tell your employer of the change so that the employer can change your status for purposes of paycheck tax deductions. If you have a health insurance plan or a pension plan, that provides benefits to your spouse, then these need to be changed as well.

✍ RELOCATION TO A NEW STATE OR COUNTRY

There is no need to change your Estate Plan for a move within the state of Florida. There is much to check out if you are moving to another state. If your attorney has your original Will (or any other original document), then unless you plan to continue with him as your attorney, you need to retrieve those original and take them with you to the new state.

You need to determine whether your Will conforms to the laws of the state of your new residence. Most states will honor a Will drafted according to Florida law, however, the rights of a spouse vary considerably state to state. If you are married and have not provided the minimum amount as required by the laws of the new state, then should you die before your spouse, your Will may be challenged on that basis. The same applies to a Trust. Many states, like Florida, require funds from a Revocable Living Trust be used to pay the minimum amount allowed by law to the surviving spouse.

If you do not have a Will, it is important to check out the Laws Intestate Succession for that state. In some states they are referred to as the *Laws of Descent and Distribution*. Each state has its own laws relating to the inheritance of property and those laws are very different from each other. Who has the right to inherit your property in the state of Florida may be different from who can inherit your property in another state. If you do not have a Will, then this is the time to think about who will get your property in the state of your new residence.

This is especially important for those who are married. The right of a spouse to inherit property varies significantly from state to state. There is a world of difference between the rights of a spouse in a Community Property state and other states. And there is even variation in the rights of a spouse from one community property state to another!

CREDITOR PROTECTION

Creditor protection is another item that is significantly different state to state. Florida is known as "Debtor's Haven" because there are so many items that you can own free from the reach of your creditors, not the least of which is your homestead — regardless of its value. Many other states have little or no creditor protection. In such states, anything you own can be lost to your creditors. If you have much debt, before moving to another state, check out what items are "creditor proof" in that state. Also determine which items can be inherited by your family free of your debts.

OTHER ESTATE PLANNING DOCUMENTS

Many states have laws directing physicians to honor a Health Care Directive, such as a Living Will, that is properly drafted in another state. Other states will not recognize a Health Care Directive unless it is drafted according to the laws of that state. But even if the laws of the state honor your Directive, consider changing your document to conform to the state of your new residence. Medical Directives vary significantly state to state. Other states may have laws that enable you to appoint someone with powers similar to a Health Care Surrogate, but the laws of the state may refer to such person as a *Patient Advocate* or a *Health Care Representative* or a *Health Care Agent*. It is best to sign a new document using the form and terminology recognized in the new state, rather than chance any confusion should you become ill and find yourself in an emergency situation.

TAX CONCERNS

You also need to check out the taxes of the new state. Each state has its own tax structure. Some states have an inheritance tax, or a transfer tax on all inherited property. If state taxes are high, you may need an Estate Plan that will minimize the impact of those taxes.

When moving to another state you need to either educate yourself about the laws of the state, or consult with an attorney who can assist you in reviewing your Estate Plan to see if that plan will accomplish your goals in that state.

✍ A SIGNIFICANT CHANGE IN THE LAW

We pay our legislators (state and federal) to make laws and, if necessary, change those in effect. We pay judges to interpret the law and that interpretation may change the way the law operates. The legislature and the judiciary do their job and so laws change frequently. Tax laws are particularly volatile. The 2001 change in the federal Estate Tax law gradually increases the Exclusion amount so that by 2010 no federal Estate Tax will be due regardless of the value of your Estate. You may be thinking that there is no need for an Estate Tax plan because you don't intend to die prior to 2010. But any certainty relating to death and taxes is false security (especially taxes, in this case). As explained in Chapter 2, the law as passed in 2001, is effective only until December 31, 2010. If lawmakers do nothing, then on January 1, 2011, the federal Estate Tax goes back into effect; and Estates that exceed one million dollars will once again be subject to Estate taxes.

And that is not the only uncertainty. Each state has its own Estate Tax structure. It remains to be seen how each state will react to the federal change. Some states may follow the lead of the federal government and increase their Estate Tax Exclusion in the same manner. Other states may see this as an opportunity to "pick up the slack" i.e., to increase their Estate Taxes, so that monies that would have been paid to the federal government will now be paid to the state.

You need to keep up with the news to learn about changes in the law that affect your Estate Plan. It is a good idea to check with your attorney on a regular basis to see if any change in the state or federal law affects your current Estate plan. And also check out the Eagle Publishing Company Web site for changes we will post to keep this book fresh.   http://www.eaglepublishing.com

GAMES DECEDENTS PLAY

We discussed the game of "hide and seek" some decedents play with their heirs. A variation of that game is the "wild goose chase." The person who plays this game is one who never updates his files. His records are filled with all sorts of lapsed insurance policies, promissory notes of debts long since paid; brokerage statements of securities that have been sold, and so on.

When he is gone, his family will become frustrated as they try to hunt down the "missing" asset. If you wish to play this game, then the best joke is to keep the key to a safe deposit box that you are no longer leasing. That will keep folks hunting for a long time!

If you do not have a wicked sense of humor, then do your family a favor and update your records on a regular basis.

Glossary

ABSTRACT OF TITLE An *Abstract of Title* is a condensed history of the title to the land. It consists of a summary of all the documents recorded with the Clerk of the Circuit Court that affect the land, including mortgages.

ADMINISTRATION The *Administration* of a Probate Estate is the management and settlement of the decedent's affairs. There are different types of administration. See *Ancillary Administration* and *Summary administration.*

AFFIANT An *Affiant* is someone who signs an affidavit and swears or acknowledges that it is true in the presence of a notary public or other person with authority to administer an oath or take acknowledgments.

AFFIDAVIT An *Affidavit* is a written statement of fact made by someone voluntarily, under oath, or acknowledged as being true, in the presence of a notary public or someone else who has authority to administer an oath or take acknowledgments.

AGENT An *Agent* is someone who is authorized by another (the principal) to act for or in place of the principal.

ANATOMICAL GIFT An *Anatomical Gift* is the donation of all or part of the body of the decedent for the purpose of transplantation or research.

ANCILLARY ADMINISTRATION An *Ancillary Administration* is a Probate proceeding that aids or assists the original (primary) Probate proceeding. Ancillary administration is conducted in another state to determine the beneficiary of the decedent's property located within that state, and to determine whether the property is taxable in that state.

ANNUAL GIFT TAX EXCLUSION The *Annual Gift Tax Exclusion* is the amount a person can gift to another each year without being required to file a federal Gift Tax Return. The Annual Gift Tax Exclusion is currently $11,000.

ANNUITANT An *annuitant* is someone who is entitled to receive payments under an annuity contract.

ANNUITY An *annuity* is a contract that gives someone (the annuitant) the right to receive periodic payments (monthly, quarterly) for the life of the annuitant or for a given number of years.

ASSET An *asset* is anything owned by someone that has a value, including personal property (jewelry, paintings, securities, cash, motor vehicles, etc.) and real property (condominiums, vacant lots, acreage, residences, etc.).

ASSIGN To *assign* is to transfer one's rights to another; for example, a contract may allow the parties to assign their rights under the contract to another person,

ATTORNEY or ATTORNEY AT LAW An *attorney*, also known as an *Attorney at law*, or a *lawyer*, is someone who is licensed by the state to practice law in that state.

ATTORNEY-IN-FACT An *Attorney-In-Fact* is someone appointed to act as an Agent for another (the Principal) under a Power of Attorney.

BASIS The *basis* is a value that is assigned to an asset for the purpose of determining the gain (or loss) on the sale of the item or in determining the value of the item in the hands of someone who has received it as a gift.

BENEFICIARY A *beneficiary* is one who benefits from the act of another or from the transfer of property. In this book we refer to a beneficiary as someone named in a Will, Trust, or deed to receive property, or someone who inherits property under the Laws of Intestate Succession.

BOND A *bond* required by the Probate Court is a written document that guarantees the Personal Representative will perform his duties as required by law. The person or company that insures the performance of the Personal Representative is called a *surety.* The value of the bond is set by the Court. The cost of purchasing the bond is charged to the decedent's Estate.

CAPITAL GAINS TAX A *Capital Gains Tax* is a tax on the increase in the basis of property sold by a taxpayer.

CAVEAT *Caveat* is Latin for "Let him beware." It is a warning for the reader to be careful.

CERTIFICATE OF TRUST A *Certificate of Trust* is a document that contains basic information about the Trust such as the date of execution of the Trust; the Trust tax identification number; the identity of the Grantor, the current Trustee, the identity of Successor Trustee and the beneficiaries of the Trust, etc. Attorneys usually prepare a Certificate of Trust to give to the bank as identification instead of giving them the entire Trust document.

CIRCUIT A *circuit* is a judicial division. The state of Florida is divided into 20 judicial circuits each with its own *Circuit Court*. Each judicial circuit covers one or more county.

CFR *CFR* is the abbreviation for the *Code of Federal Regulations.*

CLAIM   A *claim* against the decedent's Estate is a demand for payment of a debt of the decedent. To be effective, the claim must be filed with the Probate Court within the time limits set by law.

CODE   A *Code* is a body of laws arranged systematically for easy reference e.g. the Internal Revenue Code.

CODICIL   A *codicil* to a Will is an addition to a Will that changes certain parts of the Will.

COLUMBARIUM   A *columbarium* is a vault with niches (spaces) for urns that contain the ashes of cremated bodies.

COMMON LAW MARRIAGE   A *Common Law marriage* is one that is entered into without a state marriage license nor any kind of official marriage ceremony. A common law marriage is created by an agreement to marry, followed by the two living together as man and wife. Florida does not recognize such a marriage as being valid if entered into, within the state of Florida, after 1968.

COMMUNITY PROPERTY   Certain states (Arizona, California, Idaho, Louisiana, Nevada, New Mexico, Texas, Washington, and Wisconsin) have laws stating that property acquired by husband or wife, or both, during their marriage is *Community Property* and is owned equally by both of them.

CONSERVATOR   A *Conservator* is someone appointed by the Probate Court to manage, protect and preserve the property of someone who is missing, or who the Court finds is unable to care for his property because of age (a minor) or incapacity.

CONTINGENT BENEFICIARY A *Contingent Beneficiary* is an alternate beneficiary; i.e. someone who inherits if the primary beneficiary dies or loses the right to inherit.

CONFLICT OF INTEREST A *conflict of interest* is a conflict between the official duties of a fiduciary (Guardian, Trustee, attorney, etc.) and his own private interest. For example, it is a conflict of interest for a Successor Trustee to use Trust property for his own personal profit.

COURT The *Court* as used in this book is the Probate Court. When referring to an order made by the court, the term is synonymous with "judge," i.e., an "order of the court" is an order made by the judge of the court.

CREDITOR A *creditor* is someone to whom a debt is owed by another person (the *debtor*).

CREMAINS *Cremains* is shorthand for *cremated remains*. It refers to the ashes of a person who was cremated.

CUSTODIAN A *Custodian* under Florida's *Uniform Transfers to Minors Act* is a person or a financial institution that accepts responsibility for the care and management of property given to a minor child.

DAMAGES *Damages* is money that is awarded by a Court as compensation to someone who has been injured by the action of another.

DEBTOR A *debtor* is someone who owes payment of money or services to another person (the *creditor*).

DECEDENT The *Decedent* is the person who died.

DESCENDANT A *descendant* is someone who descends from a common ancestor. There are two kinds of descendants: a *lineal descendant* and a *collateral descendant*. The lineal descendant is one who descends in a straight line such as father to son to grandson. The collateral descendant is one who descends in a parallel line, such as a cousin. In this book, unless otherwise stated, the term *descendant* refers to a *lineal descendant*.

DEVISE A *devise* is a gift of real property (land, condominium, etc.) made by means of a Will.

DISTRIBUTION The *distribution* of a Trust or Probate Estate is the giving to the beneficiary that part of the Estate to which the beneficiary is entitled.

DOWER *Dower* is the right of a wife, upon the death of her husband, to a Life Estate in one-third of all real property that he owned during their marriage. This English Common Law has been abolished in most states, including Florida.

ELECTIVE ESTATE In Florida, the *Elective Estate* is the value of the decedent's Estate computed for the purpose of determining the surviving spouse's Elective Share. It includes property held in the decedent's Trust and gifts he made in excess of $10,000 made within one year of his death.

ELECTIVE SHARE The *Elective Share* is the minimum amount of the decedent's estate that a surviving spouse is entitled to receive under the law. If the decedent's Will does not provide for this minimum value, the surviving spouse can elect to take the amount provided by state law and not the amount provided in the Will. In Florida the Elective Share is 30% of the Elective Estate.

ENCUMBRANCE   An *encumbrance* is a claim or a lien or a liability that is attached to real property, such as a mortgage, or lease or a mechanic's lien.

EQUITABLE   *Equitable* is whatever is right or just. If property is distributed to two or more people equitably, then the division is not necessarily equal, but according to the principles of justice or fairness.

EQUITY   The *equity* in a home is the market value of the home less monies owed on the property (mortgages, tax liens, etc.)

ESTATE   A person's *Estate* is all of the property (both real and personal property) owned by that person. The decedent's estate may also be referred to as his *Taxable Estate* because all of the decedent's assets must be included when determining whether any Estate taxes are due after the person dies. Compare to Probate Estate.

EXECUTOR   An *Executor* (feminine *Executrix*) is a legal term found in many Wills. The terms refer to the person appointed by the Will maker to carry out directions given in the Will. In modern Wills, this term has been replaced by *Personal Representative.*

FAMILY ALLOWANCE   The *Family Allowance* is the amount set aside by the Probate Court to pay for the support and maintenance of the decedent's surviving spouse and dependents during the year following his death.

FIDUCIARY   A *Fiduciary* is one who takes on the duty of holding property in Trust for another or acting for the benefit of another, such as a Personal Representative, Trustee, Guardian etc.. A fiduciary relationship is also one that is developed out of trust and confidence. For example, an attorney has a fiduciary relationship with his client.

GRANTEE   The *Grantee* of a deed is the person who receives title to real property from the *Grantor*.

GRANTOR   The *Grantor* is someone who transfers property. The Grantor of a deed, is the person who transfers real property to a new owner (the Grantee). The Grantor of a Trust is someone who creates the Trust and then transfers property into the Trust. Also see *Settlor*.

GUARANTOR A *Guarantor* is someone who promises to pay a debt or perform a contract for another person in the event that person does not fulfill his obligation.

GUARDIAN A *Guardian* is someone who has legal authority to care for the person and/or property of a minor or for someone who has been found by the court to be incapacitated.

HEALTH CARE AGENT A *Health Care Agent* is someone who is appointed by another (the *Principal*) to make medical decisions on behalf of the Principal, in the event that the Principal is to too ill to speak for himself.

HEALTH CARE ADVANCE DIRECTIVE A *Health Care Advance Directive* is a statement made by someone (the Principal) in the presence of witnesses or a written, notarized statement in which the principal gives directions about the care he wishes to receive. The Directive could contain an anatomical gift and/or a Living Will and/or an appointment of someone as Health Care Surrogate to carry out the Principal's instructions. (FS 765.101).

HEIR   An *heir* is someone who is entitled to inherit the decedent's property in the event that the decedent dies intestate (without a Will).

HOLOGRAPHIC WILL A *Holographic Will* is a Will written, dated and signed by the hand of the Will maker himself. Many states, including Florida, refuse to admit a Holographic Will into Probate unless it is witnessed according to the laws of the state.

HOMESTEAD The *homestead* is the dwelling that is owned, and occupied, in the state of Florida, as the owner's principal residence.

INCAPACITATED The term *incapacitated* is used in two ways. A person is *physically incapacitated* if he has a physical disability. A person is *legally incapacitated* if a court finds that a person is unable to care for his person or property. Once the Court determines that a person is legally incapacitated, the judge will appoint someone to care for the person or property of the incapacitated person.

INDIGENT A person who is *indigent* is one who is poor and without funds.

IRA ACCOUNT An *Individual Retirement Account ("IRA")* is a retirement savings account in which income taxes on certain deposits and interest to the account are deferred until the monies are withdrawn.

IRREVOCABLE TRUST An *Irrevocable Trust* is a Trust that cannot be cancelled or terminated until its purpose is accomplished.

INSOLVENT A person or business is *insolvent* if more money is owed than owned, or if the person or business is unable to pay debts as they come due.

INTER VIVOS TRUST   An *Inter Vivos Trust* (also known as a *Living Trust*) is a Trust that is created and becomes effective during the lifetime of the Grantor (or Settlor) as opposed to a Trust that he includes as part of his Will to take effect upon his death.

INTESTATE *Intestate* means not having a Will or dying without a Will. *Testate* is to have a Will or dying with a Will.

ISSUE The decedent's *issue* are his descendants, children, grandchildren, great-grandchildren, etc.
See DESCENDANT.

JOINT AND SEVERAL LIABILITY   If two or more people agree to be *jointly and severally liable* to pay a debt, then each individually agrees to be responsible to pay the debt, and together they all agree to pay for the debt.

JOINT TENANCY   In Florida, a *Joint Tenancy* in real property means that each Tenant owns an equal share of the property. There are no rights of survivorship unless the deed specifically says so.

KEY MAN INSURANCE   *Key man insurance* is an insurance policy designed to protect a company from economic loss in the event that an important employee of the company becomes disabled or dies.

KEOGH PLAN   A *Keogh Plan* is a retirement plan available to self-employed taxpayers. Certain tax benefits are available such as tax deductions for annual contributions to the plan. The plan is named for its author, Eugene James Keogh.

LAWS OF INTESTATE SUCCESSION *The Laws of Intestate Succession* are the laws of the state relating to who is entitled to inherit the decedent's Probate Estate if he dies without a valid Will

LEGALESE *Legalese* refers to the use of legal terms and confusing text that is used by some attorneys to draft legal documents.

LEGATEE A *Legatee* is a person to whom a legacy (gift) is given in a Will, as compared to an *Heir* who receives an inheritance under the Laws of Intestate Succession. For simplicity we have used the term *Beneficiary* for both Legatees and Heirs.

LESSOR A *Lessor* is a person or company who leases property to another (the *Lessee*). In the case of real property, the Lessor is known as the Landlord and the Lessee as the Tenant.

LETTERS *Letters* is a document, issued by the Probate court, giving the Personal Representative authority to take possession of and to administer the Estate of the decedent.

LIEN A *lien* is a charge against a person's property as security for a debt. The lien is evidence of the creditor's right to take the property as full or partial payment, in the event that the debtor defaults in paying the monies owed.

LIFE ESTATE A *Life Estate* interest in real property is the right to possess and occupy the property for so long as the owner of the Life Estate lives. When the owner of the Life Estate dies, the property will belong to the owner of the *Remainder Interest*.

LITIGATION *Litigation* is the process of carrying on a lawsuit, i.e., to sue for some right or remedy in a court of law. A Litigation Attorney is one who is experienced in conducting the law suit and in particular, going to trial.

LIVING WILL   A *Living Will* is a Health Care Directive that gives instructions about whether life support systems should be withheld or withdrawn in the event that the person who signs the Living Will is terminally ill or in a persistent vegetative state and unable to speak for himself.

MEDICAID *Medicaid* is a public assistance program sponsored jointly by the federal and state government to provide Medical Assistance for people with low income and limited assets.

NET PROBATE ESTATE The *Net Probate Estate* is the value of the decedent's Probate Estate, less all the monies paid to settle the Estate, i.e. what is left once all valid claims and the costs and expenses of the Probate procedure are paid.

NET PROCEEDS The *net proceeds* of a sale is the sale price less costs and expenses paid to make the sale.

NET WORTH A person's *net worth* is the value of all of the property that he owns less the monies he owes.

NEXT OF KIN *Next of kin* has two meanings in law: *next of kin* refers to a person's nearest blood relation or it can refer to those people (not necessarily blood relations) who are entitled to inherit the property of a person who dies without a valid Will.

NON-PROBATE TRANSFER A *Non-probate Transfer* is the transfer of property to the decedent's beneficiary without the necessity of a Probate Procedure. This includes property that is transferred to the surviving joint owner, or property transferred to the beneficiary of a Pay On Death account.

PER CAPITA GIFT   A *per capita* gift is a gift to a group of people such that if one of them dies before the gift is given, the deceased person's share is distributed among the surviving beneficiaries.

PERJURY *Perjury* is lying under oath. The false statement can be made as a witness in court or by signing an Affidavit. Perjury is a criminal offense.

PERSONAL EFFECTS *Personal effects* is personal property that is kept for one's personal use such as clothing, jewelry, books, and other items generally found in the home.

PERSONAL PROPERTY *Personal property* is all property owned by a person that is not real property (real estate). It includes personal effects, cars, securities, bank accounts, insurance policies, etc.

PERSONAL REPRESENTATIVE A *Personal Representative* is someone appointed by the Probate Court to settle the decedent's Estate and to distribute whatever is left to the proper beneficiary.

PER STIRPES *Per Stirpes* is a method of distributing property to a group of beneficiaries. In the event a beneficiary dies before the gift is distributed, the deceased person's share goes to his descendants. If he has no descendants, the surviving beneficiaries share equally in the gift.

PETITION A *Petition* is a formal written, request to a Court asking the Court to take action or to issue an order on a given matter; e.g. a request to appoint a Guardian.

POST-NUPTIAL AGREEMENT A *Postnuptial Agreement* is an agreement made by a couple after marriage to decide their respective rights in case of a dissolution or the death of a spouse.

POWER OF ATTORNEY A *Power of Attorney* is a document in which the person who signs the document (the *Principal*) gives another person (his *Agent*) authority to do certain things on behalf of the Principal.

PRE-NUPTIAL AGREEMENT A *Prenuptial Agreement* (also known as an *Antenuptial agreement*) is an agreement made prior to marriage whereby a couple determines how their property is to be managed during their marriage and how their property is to be divided should one die, or they later divorce.

PRINCIPAL The *Principal* of a Power of Attorney is the person who permits or directs another (his *Attorney-In-Fact* or *Agent*) to act for him.

PROBATE *Probate* is a Court procedure in which a Court determines the existence of a valid Will. The Decedent's Estate is then settled by the Personal Representative who pays all valid claims and then distributes whatever remains to the proper beneficiary.

PROBATE ESTATE The *Probate Estate* is that part of the decedent's estate that is subject to Probate. It includes property that the decedent owned in his name only or as a Tenant In Common. It does not include property that was jointly with right of survivorship. It does not include property held "in trust for" or "for the benefit of" someone.

PRO BONO The term *Pro Bono* means "for the public good." When an attorney works Pro Bono, he does so voluntarily and without pay.

PUNITIVE DAMAGES *Punitive damages* are awarded by a Court to punish someone who deliberately disregarded the rights or safety of another (MN 549.20). It is money awarded in addition to *compensatory damages* which are monies awarded to reimburse the wronged person for actual losses.

REAL PROPERTY *Real property,* also known as *real estate,* is land and anything permanently attached to the land such as buildings and fences.

REGISTERED AGENT A *Registered Agent* of a corporation is someone who is authorized to act on behalf of the company and accept service of process in the event the company is sued.

REMAINDER INTEREST The *Remainder Interest* in real property is the property that passes to the owner of that Interest, once the owner of the Life Estate dies. See LIFE ESTATE

RESIDUARY BENEFICIARY A *residuary beneficiary* of a Will is a beneficiary who is entitled to whatever is left of the Probate Estate once specific gifts made in the Will have been distributed and once the decedent's bills, taxes and costs of probate have been paid. If there is more than one residuary beneficiary, then unless the Will states differently they share equally in the residuary estate.

RESIDUARY ESTATE A *Residuary Estate* is that part of a probate estate that is left after all expenses and costs of administration have been paid and specific gifts have been distributed.

REVOCABLE TRUST   A *Revocable Trust* is a Trust which can be amended or revoked by the Grantor or Settlor during his lifetime.

REVOCABLE LIVING TRUST A *Revocable Living Trust* (also known as an *Inter Vivos Trust*) is a Revocable Trust that is created and becomes effective during the lifetime of the Grantor or Settlor.

SECURED LOAN A *Secured loan* is a loan backed by property. If the borrower does not pay the debt, the lender can take the property. Car loans and mortgages are secured loans.

SETTLOR   A *Settlor* or *Trustor* is someone who creates a Trust.

SIBLING   A *sibling* is one of two or more people born of the same parents; i.e., a brother or a sister. Unless, otherwise noted, we used the term to include those who have only one parent in common; i.e. a half brother or a half sister.

SOLEMNIZE   To *solemnize* a marriage is to enter a marriage publicly, before witnesses, rather than privately as in a common law marriage.

SPECIFIC GIFT) A *Specific Gift* is a gift of a specific item, or part of the Will maker's Estate, that is made to a named beneficiary of the Will.

SPENDTHRIFT A *spendthrift* is someone who spends money carelessly or wastefully or extravagantly.

SPENDTHRIFT TRUST   A *Spendthrift Trust* is a Trust created to provide monies to a beneficiary, and at the same time protect the Trust property from being taken by the creditors of the beneficiary.

STATUTE OF LIMITATION   A *Statute of Limitation* is a federal or state law that sets maximum time periods for taking legal action. Once the time set out in the statute passes, no legal action can be taken.

STEPPED-UP BASIS   A *stepped-up basis* is the value placed on property that is acquired in a taxable transaction such as inheriting property or purchasing property (Internal Revenue Code 1012). The "step-up" refers to the increase in value from the basis of the former owner (usually what he paid for it), to the basis of the new owner (usually the market value when the transfer is made).

SUCCESSOR TRUSTEE   A *Successor Trustee* is someone who takes the place of the Trustee.

SUMMARY ADMINISTRATION   A *Summary Administration* is a simplified and/or shortened Probate procedure.

SURETY BOND   A *Surety Bond* is a bond in which a company (the *Surety*) agrees to pay if the *Principal* defaults on his obligation. For example, the Court may order the Personal Representative to be bonded for the value of the Probate Estate. If the Personal Representative does not perform his duties and the Estate loses money, the Court can require the Surety to pay for the lost funds.

SURROGATE   A *Surrogate* is a substitute; someone who acts in place of another.

TENANCY BY THE ENTIRETY   A *Tenancy by the Entirety* is the name of a form of ownership of real property held by a husband and wife. It is a joint tenancy with right of survivorship, modified by the common law concept that the husband and wife are one. With a joint tenancy with right of survivor, each joint tenant owns their own share of the property until death, when the surviving owner owns it 100%. With a Tenancy by the Entirety, each owns 100% of the property both before and after death.

TENANCY IN COMMON   *Tenancy In Common* is a form of ownership such that each tenant owns his/her share without any claim to that share by the other tenants. Unlike a joint tenancy, there is no right of survivorship. Once a tenant in common dies, his/her share belongs to the tenant's estate and not to the remaining owners of the property.

TESTATE *Testate* means having made a Will or dying with a Will.

TESTATOR The *Testator* is someone who makes and signs a Will; or someone who dies leaving a Will.

TITLE INSURANCE   *Title Insurance* is a policy issued by a title insurance company after searching title to the property. The insurance covers losses that result from a defect of title, such as unpaid taxes, or a claim of ownership of the property.

TRUST AGREEMENT A *Trust Agreement* is document in which someone (the Grantor, Settlor or Trustor) creates a Trust and appoints a Trustee to manage property placed into the trust. The usual purpose of the Trust is to benefit persons or charities named by the Grantor as beneficiaries of the Trust.

TRUSTEE   A *Trustee* is a person, or institution, who accepts the duty of caring for property for the benefit of another.

UNDUE INFLUENCE   *Undue influence* is pressure, influence or persuasion that overpowers a person's free will or judgment, so that a person acts according to the will or purpose of the dominating party.

UNSECURED CREDITOR   An *unsecured creditor* is someone who is owed money on a promissory note with nothing to back it up if payment is not made. A *secured creditor* holds some special assurance of payment, such as a mortgage on real property or a lien on a car.

WAIVER   A *waiver* is the intentional and voluntary giving up of a known right.

WRONGFUL DEATH   A *wrongful death* is a death that was caused by the willful or negligent act of a person or company.

INDEX

WEB SITES

STATE WEB SITES

138 Florida Statutes are referenced in
Guiding Those Left Behind In Florida

Each state has its own set of laws relating to the settlement of a person's Estate. The laws that are referenced in this book are very different from the laws of other states.

The author is in now in the process of "translating"
Guiding Those Left Behind
for the rest of the states, that is, writing state specific books that explain how to settle the affairs of someone who dies in the given state.

Books for the following states are now in print:
ALABAMA, ARIZONA, CALIFORNIA, CONNECTICUT
FLORIDA, GEORGIA, HAWAII, ILLINOIS, INDIANA
IOWA, KENTUCKY, LOUISIANA, MASSACHUSETTS
MARYLAND, MICHIGAN, MINNESOTA, MISSOURI
MISSISSIPPI, NEW JERSEY, NEW YORK
NORTH CAROLINA, OHIO, OKLAHOMA
PENNSYLVANIA, SOUTH CAROLINA, TENNESSEE
TEXAS, VIRGINIA, WASHINGTON, WISCONSIN

Readers of this book can purchase *Guiding Those Left Behind* for $22. This includes shipping.

To order or to check for book availability in other states call Eagle Publishing Company at (800) 824-0823.
- or -
Visit our Web site http://www.eaglepublishing.com

BOOK REVIEWS OF *Guiding Those Left Behind*

ARIZONA

Ben T. Traywick of the Tombstone Epitaph said "This book is an excellent reference book that simplifies all the necessary tasks that must be done when there is a death in the family. There is even an explanation as to how you can arrange your own estate so that your heirs will not be left with a multitude of nagging problems." "The reviewer has been going through probate for two years with no end yet in sight. This book at the beginning two year ago would have helped immensely."

CALIFORNIA

Margot Petit Nichols of the Carmel Pine Cone called it a ". . .TRULY RIVETING READ." " . . . I could scarcely put it down." "This is a book that we should all have, either on our book shelves or thoughtfully placed with our important papers."

FLORIDA

Maryhelen Clague of the Tampa Tribune Times wrote "Amelia Pohl has created a handy, self-help guide that illustrates the necessary steps that must be taken when someone dies, a guide that is easy to read, extremely clear and simple to refer to when the need arises."

NEW YORK

Saul Friedman of NEWSDAY said "And one section that should be read by readers of any age, suggests and describes how to create an 'If I Die' file to point the way to your vital papers and policies, to minimize the problems and costs for your survivors. Alas, not even you boomers will live forever."

OTHER BOOKS BY AMELIA E. POHL

How To Defend Yourself Against Your Lawyer

is a book about the unhappy experiences people have with their lawyers, beginning with that of the author AMELIA E. POHL. She became involved in a law suit and found herself in the role of client, rather than lawyer. She become concerned with lawyers who do not provide their clients with the loyalty and respect they deserve. This book is a result of those concerns.

The book is divided into chapters that cover the most common problems that take people to a lawyer: divorce, probate, criminal, personal injury, starting a business, making a Will, buying a house, etc. Each chapter tells of the misadventures of the unwary as they sought the services of a lawyer without a clue as to what they were "buying." This book is funny, sad, interesting, but most of all informative. It tells the reader how to become a savvy consumer, i.e., how to find the right lawyer for the right job. If the reader ever finds the need to employ a lawyer, he will be glad he read this book.

Copyright 2004   272 pages   6" X 9"   soft cover
$20 includes Shipping and Handling

Beyond Grief To Acceptance and Peace

AMELIA E. POHL and the noted psychologist BARBARA J. SIMMONDS, Ph.d, have written a book for those families who have suffered a loss.

What to say to the bereaved

✦ How to help a child through the loss

✦ Strategies to adjust to a new life-style

✦ When and where to seek assistance.

80 pages   6" X 9" $10 includes Shipping and Handling
TO ORDER CALL (800) 824-0823.

A Will is Not Enough. . .

Many people who have a Will think that they have their affairs in order. They believe that their Will can take care of any problem that may arise. But the primary function of a Will is to distribute property to people named in a Will. A Will cannot:

⇨ Protect your assets and limit your debt

⇨ Provide care for a minor or disabled child

⇨ Avoid Guardianship

⇨ Appoint someone to make your health care decisions should you be unable to do so

⇨ Appoint someone to handle your finances should you be unable to do so

⇨ Arrange to pay for your health care should you need long term nursing care, including qualifying for MEDICAID.

AMELIA E. POHL, Esq. has written a series of state specific books explaining how to do all of these things. This new book series is a continuation of this book. It builds on basic Estate Planning concepts introduced in Chapter 7 of this book and then goes on to introduce other, more sophisticated, Estate Planning methods. Although the topics are sophisticated, the writing style is the same as in this book. It is written in plain English. It is intended for use by the average person.

A Will Is Not Enough is now available for:
ARIZONA, CALIFORNIA, CONNECTICUT, COLORADO
FLORIDA, HAWAII, INDIANA, ILLINOIS, MARYLAND
MICHIGAN, MASSACHUSETTS, NEBRASKA, NEW JERSEY
NEW MEXICO, NEW YORK, OREGON, PENNSYLVANIA
TEXAS, VIRGINIA, WASHINGTON, WISCONSIN.

Readers of this book can purchase *A Will Is Not Enough* for $25. To check for book availability in other states call Eagle Publishing Company at (800) 824-0823.

It is the goal of EAGLE PUBLISHING COMPANY
to keep our publications fresh.

As we receive information about changes to the
federal or state law we will post an update to this
edition at our Web site.

http://www.eaglepublishing.com